Ready, Set, *Live!*

Ready Set Live!

Empowering Strategies
for an Enlightened Life

Janet Bray Attwood,
Marci Shimoff, & Chris Attwood
with Geoff Affleck

And 22 Ambassadors of Personal Transformation
Jennifer Scavina, Christina A. Beauchemin, Sergio Baroni,
Melinda Anderson, Louisa Jewell, Maggie Dillon Katz, Mayra Fernandez,
Anita Catalano, EM Richter, Katharine Bain, Michael LeValley,
Tracey Souverein, Angela Romero, Lance Rennka,
Lisa Bader, Mindy Mackenzie, Ann Calderone, Sarah Kotz,
Ayo Kenyatta Haynes, Kim Harmon, Candace Pedicord, Raven Sinclaire

New York

Ready, Set, *Live!*

Empowering Strategies *for an* Enlightened Life

Published in New York, New York, by Morgan James Publishing. Morgan James and The Entrepreneurial Publisher are trademarks of Morgan James, LLC.
www.MorganJamesPublishing.com

The Morgan James Speakers Group can bring authors to your live event. For more information or to book an event visit The Morgan James Speakers Group at www.TheMorganJamesSpeakersGroup.com.

A **free** eBook edition is available
with the purchase of this print book.

CLEARLY PRINT YOUR NAME ABOVE IN UPPER CASE

Instructions to claim your free eBook edition:
1. Download the BitLit app for Android or iOS
2. Write your name in **UPPER CASE** on the line
3. Use the BitLit app to submit a photo
4. Download your eBook to any device

ISBN 978-1-63047-660-1 paperback
ISBN 978-1-63047-661-8 eBook
Library of Congress Control Number:
2015907552

Cover Design by:
Rachel Lopez
www.r2cdesign.com

Interior Design by:
Bonnie Bushman
bonnie@caboodlegraphics.com

In an effort to support local communities and raise awareness and funds, Morgan James Publishing donates a percentage of all book sales for the life of each book to Habitat for Humanity Peninsula and Greater Williamsburg.

Get involved today, visit
www.MorganJamesBuilds.com

Habitat
for Humanity®
Peninsula and
Greater Williamsburg
Building Partner

We dedicate this book to our families and friends who have supported our journeys. Knowing that there are no mistakes in the Universe, it is our joy to offer these stories, advice, and tools to those who have been drawn to these pages.

Contents

Chapter 1   Living in the Miracle Zone   1
              Marci Shimoff
Chapter 2   Opening the Door to a New Realm of Possibility   10
              Janet Bray Attwood
Chapter 3   The Unexpected Power of Ritual   18
              Chris Attwood
Chapter 4   Back from the Brink: Relationship   27
              Rescue from a Man's Point of View
              Geoff Affleck
Chapter 5   Power Lunch   36
              Jennifer Scavina
Chapter 6   Finally! Fearlessly Me   45
              Christina A. Beauchemin
Chapter 7   Waking Up to Authentic Self-Love   53
              Sergio Baroni
Chapter 8   Love Is an Inside Job   62
              Melinda Anderson
Chapter 9   Leaving Self-Doubt Behind: Tap into   71
              the Science of Self-Confidence
              Louisa Jewell
Chapter 10   Prepare for Take-Off: Release Your Fears and Soar   80
              Maggie Dillon Katz
Chapter 11   *Basta Ya!* Enough Already! Grandma Shaman's   90
              Advice for Living a Kick-Ass Life
              Mayra Fernandez

Chapter 12   Pilgrim in Prada: How to Live a First-Class Life   99
              and Liberate Your Soul
              Anita Catalano

Chapter 13   Lost and Found   109
              EM Richter

Chapter 14   Born Confident   114
              Katharine Bain

Chapter 15   Discover the Art of Freedom—and Thrive!   122
              Michael LeValley

Chapter 16   Mother Mary's Tips for Parenting from   131
              Love, Not Fear
              Tracey Souverein

Chapter 17   How to Love Others Without Losing Yourself   140
              Angela Romero

Chapter 18   Make the Best of the Bumps on the Road   148
              Lance Rennka

Chapter 19   Treasure Hunting for Meaningful Gifts   156
              Lisa Bader

Chapter 20   Turning Your J-O-B into Your J-O-Y: 165
              Transform Your Relationship with Your Boss!
              Mindy Mackenzie

Chapter 21   Dearly Divorcing: Choose Love and Live   174
              Happily Ever After
              Ann Calderone

Chapter 22   Will He Call Me? Break Your Addiction   182
              to Unavailable Men!
              Sarah Kotz

Chapter 23   PTSD, Who Me?   191
              Ayo Kenyatta Haynes

Chapter 24   In Flows Forgiveness: How to Melt a   200
              Frozen Heart
              Kim Harmon

Chapter 25   In the Presence of Ducks: How Agreements   209
             Shape Our Lives
             Candace Pedicord

Chapter 26   Your Sacred Purpose: Put Your Personal Power   218
             and Passion to Work Now!
             Raven Sinclaire

Enlightened Bestseller Mastermind Experience   227

Chapter 1
Living in the
Miracle Zone

T he year was 1948.

Every morning, a man named Marcel Sternberger would leave his home in New York City and take the same 9:09 subway to work. One day, Marcel decided to visit an ill friend before going to work, so he took a different subway, one he'd never ridden before. The car was packed, but there was one vacant seat. As Marcel sat down, he noticed that the man next to him was reading a Hungarian newspaper. Marcel was originally from Hungary, so he struck up a conversation in Hungarian with him.

He found out that this man, Bela Paskin, had survived extreme atrocities during World War II and had ended up in a Russian work camp. After the war was over, Bela walked hundreds of miles back to his hometown in Hungary, only to find that his entire family, including his beloved wife, had been killed in the concentration camps. He was so devastated that he eventually left Hungary and made his way to New York.

As Marcel listened to Bela's sad story, it felt strangely familiar to him. Just a few days earlier, he'd met a woman at a dinner party who had told him a very similar story. He'd been so intrigued by her story that he'd written her name and phone number on a slip of paper and put it in his pocket. Marcel reached into his pocket for the paper, and asked Bela his wife's name.

Bela replied, "Well, my wife's been dead for years, but her name was Marya."

Marcel grabbed Bela by the hand and urged him to jump off at the next stop with him. Then they ran to the closest pay phone. Shaking, Marcel dialed the number on the piece of paper and when the woman answered, he asked, "What was your husband's name?" She replied, "Well, my husband's been dead for years, but his name was Bela Paskin."

Marcel turned to Bela and said, "It's a miracle. Take the phone and say hello to your wife."

I've shared this true story many times in speeches and on radio and TV interviews, and it still gives me goose bumps every time (I call them "God bumps"). But it's only one of the thousands of "miracles stories" I've read while co-authoring the books in the *Chicken Soup for the Woman's Soul* series. What I've found is that miracles are not only possible, they're happening all the time. And yet, if you're like most people, there's probably some area of your life in which you feel like you could use a miracle. Maybe it's finding your soul mate, or having a financial breakthrough, or uncovering your life's purpose. Or maybe it's as simple as being happy.

Now that one was a hard one for me. I've often said I came out of the womb with existential angst. Throughout my childhood and teens, I felt like I had a dark cloud around me. I continued to be unhappy in my twenties, thirties, and early forties, even though wealth, recognition, and even fame came to me during those years. It was only when I began studying happiness and applying what I learned to my daily life that everything turned around. By the time I was 50, I was genuinely, deeply happy—and that honestly seemed like a miracle to me.

But then something even more surprising happened. I started experiencing something beyond happiness. I began to notice that everything in my life felt like it was "in the flow." The right people were showing up at just the right time, whatever I needed was appearing out of nowhere, and miracles seemed to be happening almost every day. Wow, was that nice! I decided to do some research on miracles, and what I discovered blew me away: There's actually a formula for unleashing miracles in your life.

Now, if you're a type A person like me, you're probably thinking, "Okay, give me the formula *now*, so I can get to work creating my miracles!"

But here's the trick: You can't create miracles. According to the dictionary definition (with which I completely agree), a miracle is "a surprising and welcome event that is not explicable by natural or scientific laws and is therefore considered to be the work of a divine agency."

So if miracles are a gift from the divine, and there's no scientifically reliable way to create them, what can we do? *We can create the conditions that will invite miracles into our lives.* There are specific things we can do, a formula, to put ourselves in the flow that will allow synchronicities and miracles to show up in our lives—I call this "living in the Miracle Zone."

Once I uncovered this formula for living in the Miracle Zone, I created a course called "Your Year of Miracles" to show people how they can live miraculous lives. I've been astonished at the amazing miracles—big and small—that the thousands of people who've taken the course have manifested. The formula works!

Let me share with you three key steps in the formula, so you can start to live more and more in the Miracle Zone right away.

1. Set Your Intentions from Your Soul, Not from Your Ego

Let's break that down. First, set your intentions, that is, get really clear on exactly what you want to create in your life. And second, make sure they are soul-based intentions, rather than ego-based intentions. How do you tell the difference? Simple. When you set intentions from the realm of the ego, your body feels tension, anxiety, or fear: You feel "contracted." And what manifests in your life is struggle. You feel like you're pushing or forcing and you need to gain control or manipulate in order to get the results you want. When you try to create from your ego, it's always an uphill battle because you're working outside the Miracle Zone.

On the other hand, *when you set your intentions from your soul, the feeling in your body is one of ease and opening up* and effortless flow: You feel "expanded." This is where all possibilities and your true power are.

Fortunately, it's not hard to shift your intention from ego-based to soul-based: You just have to change how you're thinking of it and phrasing it. For example, if your intention is to lose weight, you might write: "I want to be a size 6." But that's phrased as an ego-based intention. Your ego wants you to look a certain way, maybe because you're afraid of being judged or rejected, or you're having a hard time loving yourself the way you now look. These thoughts are fear-based and coming from a place of lack, which is *not* where your power lies.

The same intention phrased in a way that is soul-based may sound something like this: "I am vital, fit, and healthy, and my body reflects the radiance I am inside."

Which feels better to you? Which inspires you? That's a soul-based intention. It's about aligning with the truth of who you are, a magnificent being with a divine spark. When your intentions come from the soul, you're in the flow of universal energy. You align with a greater force that lets things happen with ease. Your path is paved with grace—and miracles begin to reveal themselves, one after the other.

Do you have a list of goals, or resolutions, you set at the beginning of the year? Go through the list and identify which ones feel like ego intentions and which ones like soul intentions. Think about how you can shift each one, so that they all have the energy of that greater force that gets results with ease. Next thing you know, you'll find yourself in the Miracle Zone!

2. Surround Yourself with People Who Will Supercharge Your Intentions

According to the universal principal of the Law of Attraction, *Whatever you put your attention on grows stronger in your life.* Your attention is powerful and if you put it on lack and limitation, you'll manifest more of the same. But if you put your attention on what's *good* in your life, *that's* what you'll get more of.

Now, you may be doing your best to put your attention on the good in your life, but still feel thwarted in your desire to live in the Miracle Zone. If so, it could be because you're being affected by the negative or limiting thoughts of the people around you. Their thoughts may be dragging you down.

Ask yourself, "Are there people in my life who are creating negativity or resistance that might be holding me back? Are there people who, for one reason or another, might not want me to be happy and successful?"

There are numerous studies showing that matter and reality are profoundly affected not only by our thoughts, but also by the thoughts of those around us. In fact, a few years ago, Lynne McTaggart, a brilliant colleague and friend of mine, began a global movement called the Intention Experiment. This is a series of scientifically controlled experiments testing the power of intention to change the physical world. In her pilot experiment, Lynne asked a group of people in London to direct their thoughts to four targets in a laboratory in Germany. The targets were two types of algae, one plant, and one human volunteer. The people in London attempted to lower certain measurable biological processes in the four targets, solely with their thoughts. The result? Significant changes in all four targets—which means the people in London created changes in the algae, the plant, and even the human volunteers in Germany, just through their intentions!

Now Lynne has gone on to experiment with what she calls the Groups of Eight, groups of eight people each, who all put their attention on the intentions of one member of the group at a time. The miracles that these groups are unleashing for themselves are far beyond what the individuals could have created on their own, including healings, loved ones being reunited, monetary windfalls, houses selling in twenty-four hours that had been on the market for years, lost pets showing up, and more.

So, wouldn't it be wonderful to have people around you who genuinely desire your life to be miraculous? You can create this by spending more time with people who are also excited about manifesting miracles in their lives. You could even create your own Intention Experiment by getting together a group of four to eight people to see what miracles you can work for each other with your intentions—you will be supercharging each other's intentions. And then watch as your life shifts into the Miracle Zone.

3. Own Your Worthiness

To live in the Miracle Zone, you have to be willing and able *receive* miracles—you have to let them in. And for that you need to know your fundamental worthiness; you have to experience self-love. Many people, particularly women, struggle with feelings of unworthiness. Especially these days, our culture doesn't make it easy for us to love ourselves unconditionally. And we can't feel worthy of miracles without having some unconditional self-love.

Now, I'm not talking about self-esteem here. Self-esteem is, "I like myself because…" You can fill in the blank with "I'm smart," "I'm nice looking," "I'm a loving person," "I do the right thing." But all those "becauses" make self-esteem conditional. What I'm talking about is self-*love*, which is unconditional love for yourself *no matter what*, including extra pounds, mistakes made, bad choices, addictions, or whatever. It doesn't depend on your being perfect or being "good enough." It's about an unconditional acceptance of your precious self, problems and all. It's not just self-worth: I like to call it "soul-worth."

When you don't have self-love, you block miracles from coming to you because you don't feel worthy of them—you unconsciously push them away.

Want to know if you're pushing away your miracles—both big and small? See if any of these symptoms of shaky self-love apply to you:

- Do you feel uncomfortable when someone pays you a compliment? Do you immediately deflect it instead of saying "Thank you"?
- Do you have a hard time accepting gifts? Does your body tense up a bit when someone gives you something really nice?
- Do you feel obligated when people try to help you out or support you? Do you feel you have to give them back twice as much?
- Do you have a hard time acknowledging yourself and feeling compassion toward yourself? Are you often self-critical and hard on yourself?
- Do you feel guilty when things come easily to you and feel you should have had to work harder or struggled more for the good that shows up?

For most of my life, I would have said, "yes" to all the above. Self-love was not happening for me, and I lived with the consequences: no miracles. Now I see so clearly that, to live in the Miracle Zone, you need to experience your own worthiness so you can accept the good that's always coming your way.

Let me tell you how I made a big shift with this. In 1996 I was taking a workshop with the brilliant author and teacher Marianne Williamson, who has since became a good friend. I remember Marianne saying that if you make a lot of money but don't shift your consciousness to a place where you feel worthy of that money, you will invariably lose it. I remember thinking, "No way! That would never happen to me."

But sure enough, a few years later, I made lots of money—and apparently more than I felt worthy of, because I then proceeded to lose a lot of it. Ugh. Fortunately, I remembered what Marianne had said, and I quickly started working on increasing my self-love and sense of worthiness. As I did so, I not only stopped losing money, more started pouring in—and this time I was able to let it in, and keep it!

So, start noticing if you're open to receiving or if you push things away. Notice how you feel when somebody is kind or loving to you. Notice how your body reacts when someone pays you a compliment. As you're noticing your limits to receiving, ask yourself, "What could I do right now to be more open to receiving?" Then stop and listen inside for the answer. Just by putting your attention on opening up to receiving, you'll be honoring yourself and opening up the flow of more miracles in your life.

Miracles are really just the outward sign of love flowing in your heart. When you let your soul intentions lead the way and surround yourself with people who supercharge your intentions, and, most importantly, when you feel your own worthiness, you open the door to let all good things come to you: happiness, health, abundance, and love. You step into life in the Miracle Zone. And that's a wonderful place to live!

Marci Shimoff is a #1 New York Times bestselling author, a world-renowned transformational teacher, and an expert on happiness, success, and unconditional love. She's authored the international bestsellers Happy for No Reason *and* Love for No Reason *and co-authored six titles in the Chicken Soup for the Woman's Soul series. With total book sales of more than 15 million copies worldwide in thirty-three languages, Marci is one of the bestselling female nonfiction authors of all time. She is also a featured teacher in the international film and book sensation* The Secret, *and she delivers keynote addresses and seminars on happiness, empowerment, and peak performance.*

Marci's current passion is co-leading the global online transformational program Your Year of Miracles that is helping thousands of people around the world live more fulfilling, joyful, and miraculous lives. Learn more at www.YourYearOfMiracles.com.

Chapter 2
Opening the Door to a
New Realm of Possibility

Janet Bray Attwood

or twenty years she had been working tirelessly to end world hunger as the chief fundraiser for the Hunger Project. Then in 1995 she got a call from one of her largest donors: "Lynne, will you come and consult with me on a project?"

When large donors call, fundraisers listen. So, Lynne Twist traveled to South America, where this client's work was underway. There she was joined by another colleague, John Perkins, author of *Confessions of an Economic Hit Man.*

Lynne had worked side-by-side with Mother Teresa, Nelson Mandela, and Archbishop Desmond Tutu. She had raised over $150 million for the Hunger Project and trained thousands of volunteers.

But nothing she had done before would prepare her for what was about to unfold.

During her visit, Lynne was invited to participate in an ancient ritual. Sitting around a large bonfire one evening their small group was led through a series of performances by the shaman who oversaw the ceremony. As the shaman instructed them to enter their "dream," Lynne was transported into the body of a huge bird swooping and soaring over the jungle below.

As Lynne describes it, she didn't experience the dream of a bird, she actually felt she *was* that bird. She could see the trees below and feel the wind in her wings. As she continued to fly, she began to see faces rising from the jungle below.

They were strong faces. The faces of an ancient people, painted in dramatic patterns that were not easily forgotten.

As Lynne felt herself return to her human body, she was shaken. She had never had such an experience, and it was disconcerting. As the people around the fire described what had happened, all had been transformed into some kind of animal. The shaman explained that these were each person's spirit guides and through these guides they could receive messages.

However, among the entire group, only Lynne and her colleague, John Perkins, had the same experience of flying high over the jungle as a huge bird. Amazingly, John had also seen the painted faces that continued to haunt Lynne after the ceremony.

A few days later, Lynne left for Africa, where she was expected at an important board meeting. She quickly forgot about her unusual experience and immersed herself in preparations for her meeting.

As she entered the boardroom, shamans and animal spirits were the last things on her mind. There were critical issues this board needed to address, and that's all she was thinking about. As she entered the room, Lynne gasped for breath as she witnessed the faces of the male board members around the table begin to appear with the same facial designs she had seen in her "dream."

Shocked and shaken, she excused herself from the meeting and quickly exited the building, hoping that fresh air and open space would help her find some clarity to make sense of what was happening.

Eager to return home, to her husband, Bill, and the familiar hustle and bustle of beautiful San Francisco, Lynne quickly finished up her work in Africa and boarded a plane back to the U.S. Settling back into her seat, she was relieved to finally have a little time to relax.

Without any warning, the faces appeared again. Those same distinctive facial designs now appeared on the faces of the male cabin attendants and the male passengers. *What in the world is going on?* she thought.

Lynne prayed that this was nothing more than temporary burnout, hallucinations caused from all the years of traveling nonstop around the world. Nonetheless, when she got off the plane in the U.S. she wasted no time calling her friend John.

Unfortunately, he was traveling in South America, so for two weeks she had to wait patiently until he returned. When she finally reached him, the first thing John said was, "You're seeing them too, aren't you?"

The silence between them was the only confirmation each of them needed.

While Lynne was in Africa, John was trying his best to piece together why all of these faces seemed to be appearing. Through his search, he had already identified the distinctive facial designs as belonging to the Achuar people, an indigenous tribe in Ecuador with little interaction with the modern world.

"They're trying to make contact with us, Lynne. We need to take a trip to Ecuador."

It wasn't long after that before Lynne, Bill, John, and a few others made the trip to a remote area, deep in the jungles of Ecuador.

After welcoming them, the Achuar confirmed that it was indeed their intent to make contact with a few souls whose hearts were open enough to receive the invitation they were sending. The Achuar, through their contact with other tribes, had discovered that oil companies would soon be threatening their homeland, destroying everything in their path.

They went on to tell Lynne and her group the prophecy of the Eagle and the Condor.

According to the prophecy, the Eagle represents those people of the world who have used the intellect and the mind to create great technological advance and great wealth. But in the process, the people of the Eagle have become disconnected from values of the heart and the deeper spiritual values that sustain life.

By contrast, the Condor represents the indigenous peoples of the world that have used the wisdom of their traditions and connection to heart-based values to create a rich and powerful spiritual life. A life so powerful that it can make use of the unseen spiritual forces of life to create effects on the material level.

The Achuar explained that the prophecy predicted that at this time in history, the peoples of the Eagle and the Condor must come together to ensure the existence of humankind.

The indigenous people of the world need help from the people of the Eagle to secure the safety of their homelands and gain the benefits that the modern world can provide, the Achuar said.

It is equally critical that the people of the Eagle awaken from their "dream." It is time the people of the so-called civilized world recognize that their survival depends on reconnecting with the unseen spiritual forces of life and treating all aspects of the world as interconnected, interdependent parts of one whole.

From the performance of that ancient ritual, a connection between the modern and ancient worlds was created that has now had a massive impact and in the process has transformed the lives of millions of people.

From that first trip, Lynne, Bill, John, and the others who went to Ecuador created the Pachamama Alliance (www.pachamama.org).

Working with the Achuar and other indigenous tribes, Pachamama has now saved over 10 million acres of rainforest from destruction and trained more than three thousand volunteers to lead "Awaken the Dreamer" symposia in technologically developed nations.

The Inimitable Force of Ritual

Throughout history, in every culture on earth, whatever is important to that culture has been enshrined in ritual. It's not an accident that rituals are so common. They're the ways we embed ideas, concepts, and experiences that have meaning and value.

As you learned in this story, rituals also can have much more profound effects. They can provide a gateway to the world of "real magic," things our left-brain, analytical society may find hard to believe and yet which are readily accessible to all of us when we choose to be open to a different way to view life.

There is a world of unlimited possibility that most people never tap. Because she was willing to be open, even to things she didn't understand, Lynne had a profound experience that affected the whole direction of her life.

That same possibility to open up to a whole new way of being and living is open to you. Rituals are tools. If you choose to use them, they can help you unlock the door to your real purpose in life. They can make the mundane magical, and they can help you stay the course when things get tough.

Here's a little worksheet you can use to get started.

Creating Your Simple Three-Minute Daily Ritual: Reinforce Your Intention and Stay Focused on What You Choose to Create

There are seven aspects to ceremonial rituals—rituals that create a special feeling and experience when they're performed:

1. *Intention*: One part of your daily ritual will involve reading out loud the intention you set for your day or your project.

2. *Preparation and Purification*: Create a special spot in your room or office, or on your desk where you keep the elements for your ritual. Also, take a few moments before you start to clean up and wipe off your ritual space.

3. *Use of Symbols*: In your ritual space place symbols that are meaningful to you and will inspire you as you work. These could include photos of your family who will benefit from your work, special mentors or teachers you value, mementos, and anything else that will give personal meaning to your work on this project.

4. *Activating the Senses*: Incorporate fruit, flowers, scented oils, or candles and your ritual will have a deeper and more profound effect.

5. *Prescribed Performance*: Create a specific order to what you'll do during your ritual. An example would be:

    a. Prepare the space: take a moment to clean the area, light an aroma diffuser, arrange your fresh flowers, your fruit or healthy snack, and put your scarf or cloth on.

    b. Sit quietly in silence for thirty seconds.

    c. Open your eyes and read your intention for the day out loud.

    d. If you're beginning your work, write out three things you'd like to accomplish today on this project. If you're ending, list three things you accomplished.

    e. Read a quote or passage from a book that is inspiring to you and reminds you of why you're happy to be doing this work.

    f. Quietly speak out one thing you're grateful for—find something you have not expressed on previous days.

g. Speak out one thing you appreciate about yourself—again find something you have not expressed before.

h. Put out the incense and begin working on your project.

6. *Repetition*: Repeating your ritual over and over will help to ground your intention and create new neural pathways so that your work will always be connected to the intention you set.

7. *Invoking the Unseen*: This can be as simple as acknowledging that you need help to achieve the goals you've set for yourself and you're willing to accept that help from wherever it may come.

Using these seven aspects of ritual as a guide (and you do not have to include them in the order above), take a few minutes now to design your personal three-minute ritual.

From our experience, rituals like this will create specialness in your day and your work. You'll find you're more focused when you're working, and you don't obsess over your work when you're not.

For now, commit to performing the simple, short ritual you've designed at the beginning and end of day or when you begin and end a project.

Our world is at a turning point, and if you're reading this, then your life is also at a turning point. Rituals can help you individually, and all of us collectively, connect with what has meaning and value in life.

I leave you with this ancient prayer from the Vedic tradition of India, found at the end of our book, *Your Hidden Riches*, as the intention we can hold together:

May the good belong to all the people in the world,
May the rulers go by the path of justice.
May the best of men and their source prove to be a blessing.
May all the world rejoice in happiness.

May rain come in time and plentifulness be on earth.
May the world be free from suffering
And the noble ones free from fear.

Janet Bray Attwood is a visionary, a transformational leader, and a world humanitarian.

She is co-author of the New York Times *bestsellers* Your Hidden Riches: Unleashing the Power of Ritual to Create a Life of Meaning and Purpose *and* The Passion Test: The Effortless Path to Discovering Your Life's Purpose. *She and her business partner, Chris Attwood, have trained over 1,500 Passion Test Facilitators in more than fifty countries. The Passion Test and Your Hidden Riches have been featured on the* Fox Morning Show, O Magazine, Success Magazine, Time.com, Alternative Medicine, Organic Spa, *and other media around the world.*

Janet has spoken on the power of ritual and how to discover passion and purpose throughout the world, sharing the stage with His Holiness the Fourteenth Dalai Lama, Dr. Stephen Covey, Richard Branson, Nobel Laureate F. W. de Klerk, Jack Canfield, Tony Hsieh, and many others. In addition, she and Chris Attwood arranged 70 percent of the interviews done for the hit movie The Secret.

Janet is a living example of what it means to live with an open heart and mind.

Chapter 3
The Unexpected Power of Ritual

Chris Attwood

Did you know that ritual is the success secret all successful people use yet few talk about?

Simon Cowell climbs a tree daily. Actor Colin Farrell wears the same pair of boxers covered with shamrocks and "The luck of the Irish" whenever he starts shooting a new movie. British World Cup soccer player Leighton Barnes ties and unties his shoes every time he goes out on the playing field. Tennis champion Serena Williams bounces the ball exactly five times before each serve.

Are these just silly practices or is there a more profound purpose and benefit behind them?

In an article in *Scientific American* titled "Why Rituals Work," Harvard Business School behavioral scientists Francesca Gino and Michael I. Norton say:

Recent research suggests that rituals may be more rational than they appear. Why? Because even simple rituals can be extremely effective. Rituals performed after experiencing losses—from loved ones to lotteries—do alleviate grief, and rituals performed before high-pressure tasks—like singing in public—do in fact reduce anxiety and increase people's confidence. What's more, rituals appear to benefit even people who claim not to believe that rituals work.

How I Discovered the Power of Ritual

In 1981 I was the president of a secondary dealer in government securities based in Fort Collins, Colorado. I'd taken over the reins of the company when it was floundering. Recent laws had made the company's primary investment product obsolete. The systems for processing trades were so inefficient that it took seven or eight days for trade confirmations to be sent to customers. The industry standard was twenty-four hours. Not to mention that the company was hemorrhaging money.

Six months later I'd laid off three-quarters of the staff, slashed expenses by more than $300,000 per month, gotten the company back on an even keel again, and pulled together a new management team. We'd implemented a new software system so that trade confirmations were sent out within twenty-four hours on a regular basis. I couldn't change the laws, but I'd stabilized the company and created the ability to spin off other investment companies with new products.

It had been a rough and very demanding six months, so once things were going pretty well, I took off for a week to recover. When I returned, I discovered that the company's founder had brought in a consultant from New York who'd given my management team a completely new direction.

I was blown away.

After saving the company from collapse, it felt like I'd been punched in the gut. Without further ado I told the founder that since he felt his consultant could manage the company better than I could, I was leaving.

With no idea where to go or what to do, I opened my email that same day and discovered an invitation from Maharishi Mahesh Yogi, who brought the Transcendental Meditation technique to the West. "Come to India and teach the TM technique," the email said.

I called the phone number in the email and was told I'd need to be in Washington, DC, the following Monday if I wanted to participate. I packed my bags, put my house in the hands of someone who could sell it for me, and got on a plane.

After a day in DC getting a doctor's exam and being interviewed, the following day I was on a plane to Frankfurt, Germany, ending up in a 1,000+-year-old monastery in Boppard, Germany, on the Rhein River. As I walked the halls, with their arches looking out on to the central courtyard and artifacts that monks had placed there hundreds of years ago, surrounded by beauty on every side, I thought, *How lucky I was to have been pushed out of that job!*

With about two hundred other young men, I stayed at the monastery for the next month. Toward the end of that month, Maharishi came to meet with us. Sitting on a stage in an ancient hall filled with others like me, he talked about a new program he'd just launched for single men who were committed to creating a powerful, positive influence in the world. This group of men would spend their days in deep meditation, creating an influence of peace and harmony for the whole world.

For years Maharishi had encouraged scientists to find ways to measure the effects that a large group practicing the Transcendental Meditation program and the more advanced TM-Sidhi program could have on crime, hospital admissions, accidents, and even war deaths. Some studies had already been done. Today, there are over fifty studies, many published in peer-reviewed journals, showing that there is a direct connection between the size of meditating groups and reductions in these issues.

But when Maharishi spoke to us with his lilting English, which couldn't mask the brilliance of his speech, he talked about how, in the most ancient cultures on earth, these cultures understood that a portion of society needs to be dedicated to enlivening the unseen parts of life through meditation and silence. The lives of this group are immersed in routine and rituals that benefit the entire society. The connection to the field of consciousness through such groups provides a rock-solid ground on which the lives of people in that society can be lived.

Maharishi invited some of us to be part of such a group, and while some of my colleagues went to India, I soon found myself on a plane back to the United States to start a very new and different life from my days running a financial services company. My next ten years were dedicated to a life of routine and rituals—and it was among the most fulfilling and rich times in my life.

Living in simple accommodations in the center of America, every morning I awoke and went through the same set of rituals. After my morning ablutions I'd do yoga asanas, breathing exercises, and then long periods of meditation. Around noon, I'd emerge to eat a lunch of organic vegetables, take a walk, and then have a couple of hours of activity. Then began another round of rest, yoga asanas, breathing exercises, and long meditation until dinnertime. The evening was spent reading devotional literature, and then I went to bed.

I would never have chosen such a life if I hadn't been guided to it, and yet I'm so deeply grateful for that experience. The richness of my inner life created a deep sense of fulfillment that was exquisite.

Today, I'm married with three young children. My daily routine is very different, yet the power of those years spent in routine and ritual guides my life even today. And if you're open to it, routine and rituals can enrich the life of your family as well.

Defining Rituals

Before I show you how valuable rituals can be in creating a close, connected family with well-adjusted, happy children, let's define what we mean by ritual. In this context, we're not talking so much about religious rituals (although there are wonderful rituals in every religious culture), nor are we talking about superstition. We're not even talking about habits.

We all have good and bad habits.

Rituals in contrast are conscious, intentional practices you *choose* to make habitual because they improve your life. This is why all successful people have rituals (and we'll come back to those I mentioned at the beginning of the chapter before we finish).

Rituals make things real.

In every culture, whatever is important is enshrined in ritual. In Western culture, when students complete their studies, we acknowledge their achievement and their readiness to take their place in society through a ritual we call graduation.

When we elect a new leader, there is an elaborate set of rituals to recognize this leader, including a ritual called inauguration. When two people decide that they are going to spend their lives together, we acknowledge and celebrate their commitment through the ritual called a wedding.

In each case—a student entering society, installing a new leader, two people committing their lives to each other—the actual event is abstract. What it makes it real and tangible are the rituals we surround these events with.

Whatever you want in your life, make it real by creating rituals around it. Want a new relationship? Introduce rituals to support that desire. Want more money? Practice rituals that will help make that desire real. Want better health? Establish rituals to reinforce that desire. Want a rich, rewarding, nurturing family life? Introduce rituals to create the environment that supports that desire.

Building Success from the Ground Up: Rituals and Your Family

Rituals can add great value and richness to your own life, but when you make ritual an integral part of your family's life, it takes on another layer of significance. Children *love* rituals. They provide a sense of safety, reliability, and connectedness.

Rituals are easy to include in the time you spend with your children. You just need to give a little thought to when you can add ritual to some common activities. Here is one example our family uses.

While my seven-year old daughter, Sophie, and I are walking to school in the morning we have a series of fun rituals. First, she takes five minutes for her open eyes meditation. Then we play the "Thank you, God" game. Whoever says the other's name first gets to say, "Thank you, God, for…" We always include "why" we're thankful as that adds more meaning to our gratitude. Whoever has said the most "Thank you, Gods" by the time we get to school wins (of course, Sophie always wins). When we arrive at school I ask her, "Honey, what will you create today?" Then she sets three intentions for her day. At the end of the day, as part of our bedtime rituals, I'll ask, "So, what did you create today?" Then she gets five kisses for each intention that came true (both she and I love that).

Sometime ago, my wife took Sophie to school. It was a rainy, overcast day and the weatherman said the rain would continue all day. Of course, Sophie didn't know that, so when her Mom asked her what she was going to create, she said, "The sun will come out and I'll see a beautiful rainbow." Then she ran off to school.

Meanwhile, my wife was thinking, *Well, honey, that's a nice thought, but the weather forecast says the rain will continue all day, so that intention isn't likely to come true.* (Ever notice how we adults do that?)

About half an hour after my wife got home, the sun came out. When she picked up Sophie from school, she said, "Look what you created!" Of course, Sophie had completely forgotten her intention, but when it was pointed out to her, she was thrilled.

Later that afternoon, Sophie was swinging in our backyard playground with one of her friends when a beautiful rainbow appeared. Sophie ran inside and got her mom to show her. My wife was so blown away that she took a picture of it and sent it to me, as I was traveling at the time.

Did Sophie create the sunshine and the rainbow? No. What is more likely is that the innocence of her desire was aligned with the deeper functioning of nature so her intuition tapped into what was going to happen anyway.

While rituals have many very practical benefits, their greatest value is when they help to align your awareness with the functioning of nature.

The Success Principles Behind Rituals

So why do successful people establish rituals in their lives?

Part of the reason Simon Cowell climbs a tree daily is for exercise, but there are many other ways to get exercise than to climb a tree. He probably enjoys being outside in nature. But why not just go for a walk? Yet, this multimillionaire producer who has a million things to do and people wanting his attention all the time chooses to climb a tree. Could it be that this ritual allows him to feel like a kid, to just have fun and not think about all the things that are clamoring for his attention?

The success principle: Rituals can provide balance when you have a lot going on.

No doubt wearing his "lucky" boxers reminds Colin Farrell that he *does* have the luck of the Irish, and the boxers put him in a mental and emotional state where he's ready to take on the challenges of a new film. When Leighton Barnes goes on the playing field, kneels down, and unties his shoes then ties them again, he's creating a conscious separation between his ordinary daily life and his life on the field. The ritual helps him get into an emotional and mental state where he is ready to perform at his best, or in his words, the pregame ritual "does my head."

The success principle: Rituals are a way to prepare yourself when you need to perform at your best.

When Serena Williams is getting ready to serve, she knows she needs complete focus if she is to deliver her best serve. By bouncing the ball exactly five times, she brings her full attention to the ball so that when she serves she's completely present. Her ritual is part of the reason she's won thirty-four Grand Slam titles and over $60 million in prize money.

The success principle: Rituals are a way to create focus when it's critically important that you're fully present.

Your Unique Life's Design

All of us are born with a unique design for our lives. From the time you're born you are given puzzle pieces, clues to that unique design. The problem is that no one gave you the box top that shows what the finished puzzle is supposed to look like. As a result we have all these puzzle pieces and no idea what to do with them.

If life is like a river, most people spend it crashing up against the rocks at the river's edge, getting caught in the brambles and branches, getting battered and bloodied because they have no idea how to put those puzzle pieces together. Life lived this way isn't much fun.

Rituals are like navigational tools that help you move the boat of your life back into the center of the river where you're aligned with your life's unique design. Then life begins to flow as the pieces start to fall into place. Life becomes an exciting adventure, and you can hardly wait to see what's coming around the next bend.

Aligned with the flow of life, ritual becomes the gateway to a completely new world of possibilities. Those possibilities are so vast they can almost seem unbelievable.

 *Chris Attwood is co-author of the* New York Times bestseller Your Hidden Riches – Unleashing the Power of Ritual to Create a Life of Meaning and Purpose *and of* The Passion Test: The Effortless Path to Discovering Your Life Purpose. *Chris and his ex-wife, business partner, and best friend, Janet Bray Attwood, are among the leading trainers and authors in the transformational industry, having put together some of the major strategic alliances in this industry, including arranging 70 percent of the interviews for the movie phenomenon The Secret. For more on rituals and how to tap their power, visit www.yourhiddenriches.com.*

Chapter 4

Back from the Brink: Relationship Rescue from a Man's Point of View

Geoff Affleck

I looked at Lesley, my wife of almost twenty-five years, and blurted out, "I'm not in love with you anymore. I'm done."

Lesley stared at me in shock.

"How do you feel about us?" I asked, thinking that she probably felt the same way and would be relieved that I was finally talking about the elephant in the room.

Tears welled in her eyes. "I still love you," she whispered, brokenly. "Even though we haven't been intimate in some time, I still believe in us. Is there someone else?"

I tried to dodge the question: "It's not about that."

Lesley had always been the one to reconnect us when we had drifted apart over the past dozen years. But since the birth of our daughter some four years earlier and the growth of my business during the same time, we had slowly lost our emotional connection, and our physical intimacy.

Lately she'd suggested getting counseling a few times, but I had resisted—too busy with work, I said. So she'd resigned herself to the fact that this might be as good as it gets for us, for now, anyway. She consciously shifted her attention to being the best mother she could be and to working on herself by listening to teleseminars and taking courses with various spiritual teachers and healers. She often sent me links to calls she thought I'd like.

I'd also decided that this was probably as good as it gets. Although we loved each other, got along well, and enjoyed being parents together, we might as well have been housemates. While she was working on herself, I was working on my business. It was a vicious cycle, and an all-too-common one: She couldn't fulfill my physical needs until I fulfilled her emotional needs, and I couldn't give her what she needed emotionally until my physical needs were met.

A few times a year we'd each make an effort to step toward the other: a dinner date, a mini-vacation, some flowers, a thoughtful gift, or a concession to the other's preference in the event of a disagreement. Sadly, they were short-term efforts—with short-lived results.

When pressed, I'd try to talk about my feelings, but usually I couldn't find them. I'd listen to her talk about her feelings and then try to fix the problem. (Guys, take note! *Men Are from Mars, Women Are from Venus* 101: Don't try to fix the problem until you've listened for a long time and made sure you've really heard what she's saying!) Or, I'd start yawning uncontrollably whenever any sort of deep conversation raised its head, which is apparently some kind of involuntary psychological defense mechanism. Gradually, I'd started to give up trying in the bedroom, as she had years before. On the outside we probably looked like a happy couple, but we both knew the truth: It sucked to be us.

"Look at me, please. Is there someone else?"

I looked up sheepishly. "Yes."

A few weeks prior, I had begun to have feelings for another woman. She had flirted with me, and this triggered some feelings I hadn't felt for years, so I flirted back. When we talked, I felt alive and happy again. But, it turned out that there was nothing really there for either one of us, so it didn't develop into more than talking and texting. Instead, she'd begun to counsel me to talk to my wife about what was going on, and, ironically, that's what had triggered the surreal conversation Lesley and I were having that night.

"I love you," Lesley said." I really love you. Please don't give up on us."

OMG. Her words hit me like a divine revelation. She didn't just love me—she was still *in* love with me. After all this time. How did I really feel? Was I still in love with her and didn't know it?

"I don't know," I said. "I can't fake how I'm feeling."

"You owe it to us to give us another chance."

She was right. I did owe it to us. We talked all night, and all night she trembled uncontrollably as the fear of losing "us" ran through her body. I surprised myself by being present with her all night and not yawning or escaping into sleep. Then, at one point, I suddenly realized: This was emotional intimacy! And it wasn't bad. In fact, I actually liked it. I wanted more of it. I realized my biggest mistake had been not sharing my feelings out of fear that she'd leave me for sure if she knew how I really felt. Now I was so glad that I had risked it all and ripped off the Band-Aid. And now I was also really sorry for all the pain I had caused her.

A couple of days later, I had an early-morning coaching call with a client who was leaving for Hawaii the next day, and I thought, *That's it! I'll take Lesley on a vacation so we can begin healing our relationship!*

After the call, we went out for breakfast and I announced my plan. But Lesley had no appetite for food or for a vacation. She didn't want to sit on the beach, drink wine, and come back home to this. "Running away wouldn't make it any better," she said. "If we're really going to fix this, we need help."

So we went—where else?—to Google. Keywords: "spiritual couples retreats." We quickly found something that fit the bill: personalized and definitely not traditional marriage counseling, in a warm climate! We scanned the website together:

> Our couples' retreats ensure that you'll meet one-on-one (or two-on-one) with master healers and teachers. As you relax into their loving care, you'll feel the tensions and resentments melt away. You'll be transformed and you'll take home tools to continue to maintain and deepen your transformation. Call toll-free today and speak to your own Angel Guide.

As it turned out, our "Angel Guide" was much more than a spiritual salesman. In separate interviews he asked each of us deep questions about our relationship: What did we think the issues were? What did we want to create together? Then he customized a week-long retreat for us, and less than five days after I dropped the bombshell, we had arranged for childcare and booked our Soul Adventure and the flights, rental car, and hotel. There was no time to waste—our marriage was a "code red" and we were leaving for Sedona at the end of the week!

An intensive schedule awaited us. We would be there for five days and have two sessions with practitioners each day and just one day off. We'd have a total of seven sessions as a couple and two individual sessions, ranging between two and four hours each. And somewhere in there, we would eat, sleep, and integrate.

As a constant consumer of many "woo-woo" healing and self-development modalities, Lesley was excited about what lay ahead. I, on the other hand, had some trepidation. Even though I worked in the self-help industry, I was not always walking the talk or, as my colleague Janet Bray Attwood likes to say, "Being the teacher living his teaching." My biggest fear was that I would remain emotionally shut down and unable to tap into the feelings that needed to surface in order for our relationship to survive long-term. But I was determined to let go and trust the process.

We spent the next five days immersed in emotional clearings, intuitive readings, couples massages, walks in nature, and individual sessions, including an "emergency" session to accelerate the release of my emotional blocks. There was a strong focus throughout on what they called "Deepening Your Heart and Soul Connection."

Throughout these days, a common theme emerged for each of us: Mine, no surprise, was that I was emotionally shut down, probably because I grew up in Australia, where feelings are often suppressed. Aussie men aren't supposed to have "soft" emotions, so I had never learned how to recognize them or express them. Lesley, no surprise, was physically shut down, due in part to past trauma. The skilled practitioners helped us understand the choices we had made in response to our past conditioning and start to help us free ourselves of those choices. It was amazing! Very soon, we began to reconnect emotionally and physically in ways we had thought we had lost.

We also discovered some important things about each other that have hugely improved our communication. For example, during our time hiking among the red rocks and vortexes on Day 2, our guide took us through Dr. Gary Chapman's "Five Love Languages Test," a thirty-question quiz designed to help you understand what you need in order to feel loved. There are five different love languages:

- Words of affirmation
- Quality time
- Receiving gifts

- Acts of service
- Physical touch

Not surprisingly, Lesley's number one Love Language is quality time and her number two is acts of service. My number one is words of affirmation and my number two is physical touch. No wonder we weren't connecting: We were speaking completely different love languages and didn't even know it! We started to feel closer as soon as we started doing whatever made the other feel loved. It was so simple, but it worked like magic.

Another great tool we learned is the Enneagram Personality System, a psychological tool with roots in sacred tradition that's been scientifically validated by Stanford Medical School. The system describes nine personality types, such as the Perfectionist, the Giver, and the Performer, and how they interact with each other. Each type has different ways of thinking, feeling and acting, and knowing about them can make relationships easier and closer.

For example, I'm a type 9, the Mediator, and Lesley's a type 4, the Romantic. Types 9 and 4 are both relationship-oriented, caring, and empathic, which is true for us. Where we've had trouble is that Mediators are oriented toward others and like to avoid conflict (definitely true for me), whereas Romantics are more self-oriented and like to go to emotional extremes to feel alive. Just by learning more about each other's operating systems, we've been able to make adjustments and avoid the pitfalls we so often fell into in the past.

While our relationship has benefited from these two tools, for me the most profound shift has come from an emotional exercise we learned called breath work. This deep-breathing practice brought me to places I can't usually go. Angry places. Sad places. Remorseful places. Joyful places—even blissful places. Breath work now allows both of us to experience a wider range of emotions or, as our Sedona guides call it, "full-spectrum emotions." And, for Lesley, this technique helped her to release her past trauma, and it still does today.

A few weeks after our return from Sedona we went on a two-day retreat to an oceanside cabin, specifically to revisit breath work. During my session, after I released much stuck anger and frustration via the f-word, blissful waves washed through me again and again. I cried for all the pain I had caused my wife. I cried for the incredible love I felt for our precious daughter. I cried for the happiness I felt for our rekindled relationship. And most of all, I cried for the joy I felt because I could finally *feel*, period.

So what did I learn that may be of use to other men (and women) who find themselves in what looks like a loveless marriage?

- I was still deeply in love with my wife and just didn't know it. If I had run off with someone else, it probably wouldn't have lasted because I would still have been be the same person. It would have been the classic "same guy, different woman" syndrome. Watch out for that!

- Relationships are really a mirror reflecting back what's inside yourself, and, much as you may want to, you can't run away from yourself. Do the inner work and the outer world becomes a different place, a place you don't want to leave.

- Be honest, vulnerable, and authentic. Get out of your comfort zone and lay it all on the line. Every time I put myself out there emotionally, Lesley met me there, creating a safe place to express myself. If it's harder for your partner to do that, try being the one to meet her and create a safe place for her.

- I realized that I actually could have it all. Emotional intimacy is not to be feared—it's to be sought after and embraced. A whole new world opens up when your feelings are flowing. The physical intimacy I craved is now being fulfilled both physically and by this newfound emotional intimacy. I can honestly say that our love life is better now than it was, *even when we were first dating back in '88!* I swear to God! It's matured to the point where we now feel like we really do have it all.

The amazing thing is that just a couple of months ago we were in a relationship standoff. It was like we were at opposite ends of a field saying, "You go first." "No. *You* go first."

What we discovered is that, when we *both* mustered the courage and humility to move toward each other at the same time—and also find help for the issues we hadn't been able to resolve on our own—our relationship began to flourish in ways I hadn't even known existed until now.

I had thought that all was lost if you lost that loving feeling. Now I know that all is lost only until you discover that loving feeling within yourself, for yourself and all creation, and then share that feeling with someone else. When you do that, you make a deep connection that's better than anything else on earth. When you've got that, my friend, claim it as your birthright and enjoy the fantastic new life you're living.

Resources

- To find your Love Language, go to www.5lovelanguages.com.
- You can discover your Enneagram personality type through one of the various online tests or by consulting a certified Enneagram teacher.
- To try out breath work, I recommend having at least one session with a trained facilitator to learn the proper technique. And then it's always good to have someone experienced at your side to guide you through it.

Geoff Affleck is passionate about helping contemporary thought leaders and self-help authors grow revenues and expand their audience. He is the *#1 best-selling co-author of* Enlightened Bestseller: 7 Keys to Creating a Successful Self-Help Book *and* Breakthrough! Inspirational Strategies for an Audaciously Authentic Life. *As a founding facilitator for the Enlightened Bestseller Mastermind Experience, Geoff shares his online marketing expertise with aspiring self-help authors and speakers.*

Geoff earned his MBA from the Schulich School of Business in Toronto. Born in Melbourne, Australia, he now lives on Vancouver Island, British Columbia, and enjoys yoga, wilderness camping, kayaking, and spending time with his wife, Lesley, and daughter, Skyla.

Learn more about Geoff at www.enlightenedbestseller.com and www.geoffaffleck.com.

Chapter 5
Power Lunch

Jennifer Scavina

I was taking in the room—a beautiful New York City restaurant, bustling with men in business suits and well-heeled women, many drinking red wine in lovely large glasses. I was waiting for my long-time friend Jacob to arrive and wondering what was going on with him. When he had texted to ask if we could meet for lunch in the midst of our busy lives, he wrote, "If you can make the time to see me, it would be good. I could really use some help."

Was it business related? I wondered. Both Jacob and I had achieved a certain amount of success in our careers, and from time to time, we'd help each other with decisions, contacts, and advice. Or was it something else?

Just then, Jacob entered the restaurant. A handsome, confident man, he smiled at the hostess and waved at me. Despite the smile, I sensed he wasn't okay—and that it wasn't work related.

Jacob took in the other tables as he crossed the room and joked as he greeted me that this must be the latest version of a power lunch. "We're having wine," he said, "and a power lunch of our own." Those words would stay with me long after that day.

After we'd consulted our menus and been served our wine, Jacob took a long sip and said, "I'm so glad you're here. I really needed to see you and tell you that I think this one is over, too."

I immediately knew what he meant: "This one" referred to his marriage to Kathleen, his third wife. Ironically, I had often prayed that Kathleen would be "the one" for Jacob. Kind, intelligent, pretty, and loving, she was a wonderful person, and I felt that the love they shared was real. But here sat Jacob, with a large tear threatening to spill from his eye before he brushed it away with a finger.

"It's just like the others: I can't make a go of it. Maybe thinking I could have it all was crazy? You're always reminding me to count my blessings and be grateful. Maybe my blessings are just wrapped up in health, my homes, my lifestyle…Maybe to have all of this and a love that lasts forever is asking too much. Some people are meant to have 'the love of their life,' like you found Nick," he said, referring to my husband. "But maybe some aren't. I mean, maybe it's too much to ask for, on top of all of this amazingness, you know?" he said, gesturing to himself and trying to lift the mood with a joke and laugh. But with that little laugh, a tear did manage to fall.

I shook my head, but he already knew that I didn't agree. He pushed on, almost angrily, "You know, not everyone sees the world like you do—talking about God and love and life's meaning—and somehow not making it seem too weird." I remembered him telling me years ago that he found it interesting that a person could weave God and faith into almost any setting and conversation—and even more interesting that people didn't seem to mind it.

"Not everyone can live that way, Jennifer. Not everyone can see good and meaning in life, even in the dark times, like I've seen you do. I remember your heartbreak when you buried your father, for instance, but more importantly, I remember the peace flowing out of you. I've been thinking a lot about this lately, and I want to know how you do it. I need you to teach me how to live that way."

I smiled, finally able to get a word in. "So, you want me to teach you how to live a happy life—over lunch and before we both go back to our busy lives and schedules?"

"Exactly!" he said with a laugh—but he wasn't joking.

I closed my eyes, said a prayer, and knew this was a chance to really help Jacob live a better life.

"If you really want my help, you'll have to *do* what I say, not just hear the words. I can't guarantee the outcome for you and Kathleen, but in a way, it won't matter. If you really do what I share with you, it will all be okay—in fact, way better than okay! And I know we've been friends for what feels like forever and you think I'm special, but this isn't about being special. This is something every person can do; it's a way every person can live."

Jacob broke in. "Before you tell me anything too weird, I have to ask: Does Nick know about this?" I couldn't help laughing, because Jacob knows my husband's very down to earth.

"Of course, Nick knows," I responded. "It's a big part of why we have such a beautiful relationship. Don't worry, it isn't that weird, and it's easy if you just do it."

The Starting Point

After our meal was served, I began sharing with Jacob my deepest beliefs and understanding about how life works. "We have to start with God— Spirit, Higher Power, whatever you want to call it. We don't have time over lunch to negotiate the existence of God, but I'm telling you without doubt that a spiritual realm exists, and it is more real than anything you think is tangible.

"In every breath and scenario of your life, you are connected to God, grounded in and surrounded by His love and power. Maybe you've never been aware of it, but think of a house that is completely wired for electricity—with no lamps plugged in. A lamp is never going to work unless it's plugged into a power source. In the same way, our lives will never be what they could be if we aren't plugged into our power source: God.

"So," I continued, "how do you get there? It starts with quieting your mind and opening to your spirit. This spirit of yours is connected to God—it's what led you to send that text and to have this conversation. It's what leads people to pick up books that cross their paths—an example of being nudged and guided by God to pay attention, so that life can become beautiful and miraculous.

"Keep in mind that your brain is an incredible computer that serves you, but it's not your spirit. If you ask your mind questions, it will always have an answer—but your mind will never be able to steer your life along the path you're meant to follow for your happiness. That direction comes from your spirit and your connection to God.

"So from now on, you need to start your days in silence. Even if it's just for a few minutes, things will change. Find a quiet private place, sit still, and be silent. Quiet your mind and breathe in with what I call a *knowing that God is there with you.* Imagine that God, this Higher Power, loves you more than anyone has ever loved you and wants only your highest good and happiness. Tell that to yourself and then sit within that loving space. At the end of the time, say and feel, 'Thank you, God, for always being with me.'

"I usually end my time with a prayer from *A Course in Miracles*: 'Where would You have me go? What would You have me do? What would You have me say and to whom?' I don't try to answer that, or hear an answer, I just know that God will go with me in every breath and step of that day.

"Something else you might want to write down, memorize, and call to mind often is my favorite line from *A Course in Miracles*: 'If you knew Who walks beside you on this path that you have chosen, nothing would be impossible and all else would be possible.'"

I paused while Jacob wrote it down. "It's one of the greatest truths of life: If you really knew God was with you in every moment, your life would completely change. When I'm able to remember this, my life works perfectly.

"Next comes what I call the questions. Ask them internally, but more importantly, ask them of God. When your mind is quiet, you will get an answer to anything you ask. This might not make sense now, but stay with me and you'll get it.

"The first and most powerful of the questions is this: What does love look like, for all involved, in this moment? Keep in mind that you're asking this of God and of yourself. The more you ask that question, the more you'll find your entire life changing for the better. Because in essence your entire life will be guided by God and by love.

"I'm not exaggerating when I say I ask that question hundreds of times each day—even when I'm getting a phone call. The answer might tell me that it will be a draining call or simply something that can be left for voice mail. Or I might ask it when I'm feeling tired from work, or I've been traveling and am wondering about making a good dinner for the family. The 'for all involved' part means that it has to be a loving thing for me as well, so the answer on Monday might be to make dinner, but on Tuesday to order out!"

I paused and asked, "Is this making sense?"

Jacob said, "I think so, but what about relationships? You know how great I am at those," he added with a smile. This time I noticed it was a genuine smile, and I inwardly thanked God for it.

"Okay," I said, "I have another question just for that—to help any and all relationships!"

Miraculous Relationships

"Think of a time in your life when you had a disagreement with someone. It could have been with Kathleen or anyone, and it doesn't have to be about something big—just a time when there were hurt feelings between you and someone.

"Typically, people will apologize after an argument and say they didn't mean to hurt each other's feelings. But here is the trick: At the moment hurt is recognized and apologies begin, there's a question that might be asked: 'I know we weren't trying to hurt each other, but were we intending to love each other in that moment?'

This might not seem big at first, but if you ask this one question in every interaction in your life, it will change everything. It might seem too much to ask ourselves to always *be* loving—that just doesn't work— but it isn't too hard to always be sincerely *intending* to be loving, and that profoundly changes where we're coming from. Ask yourself, 'Am I intending to love this person and myself in this moment?' and you will get answers that guide you, literally changing your life. You can ask this when dealing with your wife or family member, but also with a waiter or grocery clerk or the man sitting next to you on the bus. It's not difficult—it really just takes a little practice to remember to *intend to come from love.*"

"I can't decide if that sounds great or exhausting!" Jacob said. I assured him that it makes life so much more enjoyable and even brings about miracles.

"It can also protect you," I said. "I can tell you stories about scenarios where I knew, most definitely, that a person didn't have good intentions toward me. Yet just by holding that loving space, things changed. Or I'd be prompted to silently bless the person but stay away from him or her.

I've had times when I would be prompted to ignore specific negative behavior and trust that it won't last forever. This is more useful than you can imagine."

"But how can you do that in a marriage?" Jacob asked. "You have so many different issues to deal with."

"You both have to give it a try, and I bet Kathleen would love to. And if not, you may or may not be able to succeed on your own. It's ideal to find someone who is willing to ask the 'love intention' question with you. If you have a partner who is willing to live a life *intending to love,* then you are more than halfway to an incredible relationship. Obviously, we're human and we'll always do things that hurt each other, but if we're coming from a place of love, those things will be so limited or unimportant that they won't hurt the relationship. That's why my marriage to Nick is so special: We live our lives connected to God and *intending* to love each other."

"I want that!" Jacob said. "I'll definitely do this and see if Kathleen will, too."

"That's great!" I said. "And the third thing I think works great is to make lists—mental or written—of things that you love and appreciate about the person. If you do this often, the small, petty things that can come up in your relationships will literally go away.

"For instance, let's say Kathleen forgets to pick up your dry cleaning, and for a moment, your mind is tempted to run with thoughts like, 'Hey, she doesn't have a job!' and 'Isn't that the *least* she can do for me since I work so hard?' But if you've been thinking about the things on your list, you'll think of her being a loving, fun, and gentle person and your annoyance about the dry cleaning will seem silly and literally disappear.

"And those lists can also help you know if you're with the right person. As you create lists of Kathleen's characteristics—what you admire and appreciate about her—if you keep coming up short, you might actually be with the wrong person. This is best to use when you're dating to help you notice early on if there's a true connection to what you hold as valuable."

We had finished eating, so I said, "I have so much else to share, and I will in the future, but we're running out of time. Just trust that if you actually do these few things, your life is going to completely change and feel miraculous."

"You're like a mystic!" Jacob practically yelled across the table.

I laughed. "I'm not a mystic! The only thing that's different about me is that I consciously try to stay aware of God and do these simple things every day. When any of us consistently does this, things shift, and we get answers because our connection to God is clearer. We'll even see things differently that, on the surface, seem not to be good, because we have a trust in God and a relationship with God. Does that make sense?"

"It does," Jacob said. "I'm a little nervous but also excited to try to live this way." He paused. "But, will this really work for *anyone?*"

"Absolutely!" I said. "If you do this, it can't *not* work—and that's true for anyone and everyone. You'll see the miracles and feel the joy as you go along."

As we parted outside the restaurant, Jacob gave me a huge hug and said, "Now *that* was what I call a power lunch."

Jennifer Scavina is managing partner and senior vice president of EGR International, an engagement agency providing Dow Jones and S&P 500 companies expertise in the areas of engagement, performance improvement, marketing, and motivation. She is also co-founder of Advancing H, a consulting firm providing systematic and proactive approaches for individuals, families, organizations, and academic institutions to pursue and achieve higher levels of success.

With over twenty years of business success—and many more years in the study and pursuit of spiritual practices—Jennifer offers valuable insights and approaches to all aspects of life and shares many of these in her forthcoming book, Everyday Sage.

To learn more about Jennifer's work and initiatives, visit www. EGRInternational.com and www.AdvancingH.com.

Chapter 6

Finally! Fearlessly Me

Christina A. Beauchemin

I couldn't stop thinking about how I felt as he drove away. It was like being cold from the inside out, the kind of cold that digs down with cruel fingers, right into the bones and cartilage, cooling the blood and freezing time. I went to bed and tried to sleep, but sleep wouldn't come.

It had been a blind date. He arrived first, so the maître d' took me to meet him in the bar, which was crowded and rowdy. I was in jeans and a pair of knee-high boots, topped by a lacy blouse and a feminine gray sweater, my curly hair hanging loose over my shoulders.

"Hello, I'm Christina," I said, shaking his hand with a smile. He was a fairly nice-looking guy. He wore a dark suit with a bright red tie that appeared to be just a bit too tight around his neck.

"It's nice to meet you, Christina." He introduced himself and asked, "Would you like a glass of wine?"

I nodded. "Sure. That would be nice." I had no expectations, and I enjoyed the evening as we shared a warm booth and a lovely dinner. He revealed that he owned a successful restaurant chain and was a pilot for a local politician.

"My dad's a pilot, too," I said. "I love to fly." I asked for details on his plane. Later he shared the story of his wife's death only months earlier.

"I'm so sorry," I said when he revealed that they had been high school sweethearts who married at seventeen. "I can't imagine." The conversation flowed and it became clear as the evening rolled on that he was a nice enough guy but maybe not my type.

The wind was on the attack as we left the restaurant, ice crystals stinging my cheeks. I pulled my coat tighter to my body and said, "Wow, sometimes I hate living here."

"I hear you," he said, shivering in his leather coat. "Maybe I'll head south for a couple of weeks. Business is slow right now, and I could use some time away." His brisk step took him quickly to his Mercedes-Benz as I hurried to keep up. He pulled on his thick leather gloves, tightened his scarf, pulled out his key.

"Maybe I'll see you again sometime," he said with a wave before he jumped into his car. The bright taillights flashed and he drove off.

I stood in the cold, rooted to the spot, the wind tearing at my scarf as I watched the turn signal flash and the car turn right, then disappear. I felt breathless; like someone had punched me, hard.

I walked to the shadows where my Honda waited, then drove home to pull on thick pajamas and crawl into bed. Even my electric blanket couldn't relieve the chill that had settled in as I stood in the wind, watching the taillights grow smaller. Two hours passed while I tossed and turned until I finally gave up the idea of sleep.

I climbed out of bed, not sure what to do with myself. It was too dark and cold to take a walk, and I didn't feel like having a cup of tea. I wandered into the bathroom; the reflection in the mirror revealed chapped cheeks and red eyes. Generally, I'm not someone to let something like this bother me, but for some reason, I couldn't stop replaying the scene over and over in my mind with a background loop of "Maybe I'll see you again sometime."

Hannah, my faithful companion for over sixteen years, whined and nudged my hand. It was unusual for me to be up so late, and dogs notice these things.

"What is it about me, Hannah?" I asked. "Why do some people think it's okay to treat me like I don't matter?" I ran my hands over her head as her soulful eyes met mine. Aggravation welled up in a quick burst. "And why do I even care? He was totally not my type." I sighed and for a second my shoulders sagged. Then anger flared, replaced in the next moment by self-doubt. "I guess it's my own darn fault," I said. "I think I talk too much." I looked back at Hannah, "Do you think I talk too much, girl?"

Hannah wagged her tail, which made it easier to force a smile in the mirror, as was my habit when trying to make myself feel better. "Maybe if your teeth were straighter," I told myself, running my finger over my front teeth, "and your hair not such a mess." I made a silly face as I flattened the unruly curls that were tangled from tossing and turning. I released a frustrated sigh. "Who does he think he is?"

I stared into the mirror. After a minute or so, I got the strangest feeling. I had a sense of something that made me lean in. I realized that I was looking deeper into my eyes than I had ever looked before. I was no longer just noticing the dark-blue outer rims of my pupils and the green and yellow irises dotted with brown specks. It was as if a force I didn't understand was pulling me in, downward, further and further into my reflection.

And then it happened.

I drew in a deep breath of surprise. It was right there, just beyond the green of the eyes. And it was beautiful. It was not only beautiful, it was so amazing that it blew me away.

I wish I could find the words to describe to you exactly what I saw there. I've tried a hundred times but the only thing I can say is that the being there, looking back at me from that mirror, is magnificent. I was staggered by the realization. I was seeing myself, my real true self, for the very first time. It was a life-changing moment that I wanted to hang on to.

In the very next breath, a thought occurred to me. I knew, with a certainty I had never felt before, why my date drove off with just a flip of his leather glove, leaving me in the cold, shadowy parking lot. I sat down on the edge of the tub to keep my knees from buckling. It was as clear as the nose on my face.

If I had never truly seen myself, how could I expect anyone else to see me?

Now I'm not talking about my eyes, my nose, my hair, or the other parts that make up a face or a body. I'm talking about what makes me who I am. I knew I needed to hear the words, so I stood up and looked back into the mirror. Then I said, "If I have never truly seen myself, how can I expect anyone else to see me?"

With those words, I got it. I fully understood the power of the gift I had just received, and I burst into tears. At first they were tears of sadness. All these years gone without seeing this wonderful woman who was me. Years of carrying a deep-down fear that I wasn't good enough. But it was only a matter of seconds before those tears turned to tears of joy for the future that had just opened up. It was after midnight, but I picked up the phone. My best friend was always up late.

"How was the date?" she asked. I gave her a brief rundown and finished with, "He didn't even walk me to my car."

"Are you serious?" she asked.

"Yes," I said. "And so, you know what I realized tonight? I realized that I deserve better than that." I had never said that, not once in my life. It was my habit to make excuses for other people, but I knew that, from this moment forward, I was never going to be the person I was even five minutes before.

So what did I do with this amazing revelation? Well, I'll tell you what I didn't do: I never once returned to that woman standing in the cold, watching the taillights grow smaller. Instead, I came up with a plan for myself that developed into a process that I will share with you here. And this will be useful even if you are a strong, secure person who just happens to have a moment of insecurity now and then.

See It Yourself!

I invite you to spend several quiet moments a day really looking into your own eyes. You don't need big chunks of time. Just a few stolen moments here and there will get you used to the practice. Be sure to focus on what is behind your eyes and not on your features. This is about looking past the exterior our culture puts so much focus on to see what's inside. Use your inner guidance. Consider what it feels like when you come to that moment of falling in love with someone else. It's the same type of sensation.

If nothing happens, no worries. Look again tomorrow. Don't give up. Nothing that is amazing happens overnight. Remember that the seeing is more of a feeling than a specific visual event. And have no fear: You will see it—maybe not today, but in time.

Find Yourself a Reminder

When I woke up the next morning, I knew it was essential that I keep something nearby to remind me of that moment of revelation. It was now clear that the person who had been most unkind to me during my lifetime was me. I was famous for standing in front of the mirror on any given day, criticizing my appearance and my actions. But that day I made a promise to myself that I would never do it again.

It takes time and attention to change an ingrained pattern, so I decided I needed to find something that would act as a reminder of the new pattern I wanted to create. I wasn't sure what I was looking for as I combed the small department store near my home, but I found it. It was a small, stuffed toy: a gray rabbit with a suction cup on the back.

I went back to my house, unpacked the rabbit, licked the suction cup, and stuck it right on my bathroom mirror. That rabbit was my prompt for the next two years to remind me that, whenever I looked in the mirror, for any reason at all, I was to say, "You are amazing." Next to the rabbit, I posted a 3×5" card with the words written out.

When I first started this practice, I felt ridiculous. As time went on, though, it became both easy to say and easy to believe. And the interesting thing I learned about the rabbit is that in many cultures, it's the rabbit that leads seekers into the nether regions of their fears. It's the rabbit that helps them face those fears.

Try this yourself! Find your own reminder to look within, and post your message to yourself on the mirror. And there's more you can do. Before my breakthrough day, I had been practicing some other simple techniques for a few years. Here are two that I promise will deepen your vision.

Notice Who "I Am"!

I've developed a regular practice of making what I call "I am" statements while stretching in the morning. Using "I am" statements takes your focus off of your problems, your children, the dirty laundry, or anything else that may creep into your mind. I alternate my statements, depending on what's going on in my life, but generally I use, "I am. I am love. I am light. I am deserving."

Find a time each day when you can focus a few minutes on you, and just repeat the words easily, with one little twist: Each time you say "I," let it resonate throughout your being. Don't clip the sound. Think of the word "sigh" but say "I," and you'll understand what I mean. Hold on to it. Feel it. Close your eyes and let your inner presence feel the attention. Take deep breaths and feel your muscles relax.

Five minutes is enough, at any time that works for you, but it does need to be done regularly, every day if possible. In those few minutes, you are opening yourself to the Divine within. I needed to remind myself every day that I am deserving. You may need to work on something else. Make the practice your own.

Every Imperfect Moment Is Perfect!

Life is a challenge most days for most people. And that's wonderful! These challenges help you grow into the person you are intended to be. Some days I'm so tired I can't even think about taking five minutes for my "I am" statements. I have days when I want to put my head under the pillow and leave it there for a week. And I don't think I'm all that different from anyone else. We all have those moments. And that's okay.

The key is to remember that every moment, no matter how imperfect it seems, is perfect for what it is. When I'm overcome in a stressful moment, I've learned to remind the wonderful woman I met in the mirror on that cold February night, that it's okay. It's life! I invite you to do the same. I'm not saying it's easy. But take a deep breath, go within, and say, "This is all perfect." Breathe out and smile. Take another deep breath and repeat if necessary. Releasing the energy this way is soothing as it lets fears slip away. This, too, will become a habit when practiced regularly.

• • •

In that moment in front of the mirror, I understood that we are all born magnificent. I also realized that it's up to each one of us to recognize it and to embrace it. The evolution of the human spirit is beautiful and amazing, even in its smallest victories. Be open every day to the kind words of others, even if they seem insignificant. Love yourself enough to take in the compliment, the "thank you," the kind note or email. Don't doubt the sincerity—it's true!

Then, whether you feel it or not, plant your feet solidly on the ground, raise your hands over your head, tip your head back, and proclaim, "I am fearlessly me!" Make it so!

 *Christina A. Beauchemin is an entrepreneur, a sister to eight brothers and two sisters, a mom to two grown boys, and a wife and partner to her best friend, the one she met just seven weeks after the revelation in the mirror! She is the creator of Fearlessly Me!, a program for those who feel they are not being seen or are plagued with self-doubt and underlying fear. Fearlessly Me! provides tools for "breaking through" the mirror to find the magnificent being within, just waiting to be seen.*

Christina and her business partner, Karen Carey, would love for you to visit their website at Iamfearlesslyme.com, or you can email Christina at Christina@Iamfearlesslyme.com. They're interested in hearing your stories!

Chapter 7

Waking Up to
Authentic Self-Love

Sergio Baroni

I t started with a strange ringing in my ears. At first I ignored it, thinking it would go away on its own, but it just got worse. In the middle of the third night of incessant ringing, I woke up in a sweat, feeling nauseated, with the room spinning wildly and a high-pitched whine in my head like a dentist's drill. I discovered I couldn't stand up without falling over, so I lay in bed, struggling with the constant urge to vomit. Every minute was agonizing, and I couldn't make it stop. I felt terrified and out of control, like a man clinging to a life raft at night in a stormy sea.

In the morning, a friend rushed me to the hospital, where I was diagnosed with Meniere's disease, a severe dysfunction of the inner ear. The doctors told me that the condition was incurable, and I would continue to have these unbearable symptoms and probably lose most, if not all, of my hearing within a few years.

I was devastated. I felt helpless…terrified…alone. Was my life really becoming a living hell? How could that be, when I had just had a taste of heaven?

I had just gotten back from a week-long trip in the wilderness where I'd worked with a dozen people to help them discover their life's purpose. One starry night in a red rock canyon along the Colorado River, I'd had a transformative experience of my own. I was sitting in a natural hot spring with our group when, suddenly, my whole sense of self shifted. It was as though my heart and my eyes became one, and I was able to look at each person and "see" into their soul and perceive their beauty, goodness, and unique purpose. I felt magical and powerful and so grateful that I had been graced by a force greater than myself to bring more good into the world.

I returned home from that trip feeling ecstatic and deeply fulfilled—and kind of amazed at myself for having had this great experience. I remember wondering how anything could ever top it, and marveling at what fantastic karma I had.

And now this?

When I was released from the hospital a few days later, there was little improvement in my symptoms, and I had already had significant hearing loss in one ear. I quickly fell into a depression and was plagued with horrible feelings of dread and shame. What had I done to deserve such a fate? Was this some kind of cruel cosmic joke that the universe was playing on me? Had I been stupid to be so happy? I had been praying for help since the symptoms started, but my prayers had not been answered. I felt rebuked by God.

I lay in bed for weeks because I didn't have the balance to stand or walk. I looked forward to sleep as my only escape from the torment. I lost all sense of normalcy, let alone joy. For the first time in my life, I began to have suicidal thoughts. I felt a strange kinship with the countless people who wanted out from a life of hopeless misery.

Then one morning, out of the depths of despair, a question popped into my mind: If, indeed, I would have to suffer terribly and without relief until I eventually became deaf, what, if anything, would still make my life worth living?

This wasn't a rhetorical or theoretical question. I had to know; my life depended on it. To my surprise, a clear answer followed: As long as I could give and receive love, my life would always be meaningful and worthwhile.

I knew this was true, deep down in my bones, and as I lay there, tears came, and I felt huge relief. I knew that, no matter *what*, I would be okay, as long as I could feel and share love.

In that moment, I became devoted to love as I understood it. And I knew it had to start with love for myself. But it was clear that this love wasn't about building self-esteem; it went much deeper than my ego. And it wasn't just love for me; it had to be love for everyone and everything.

At first I didn't know how to find this kind of love, but soon I started noticing that I was speaking to myself very tenderly, with lots of kindness, patience, and encouragement. This was something new for me, and it felt amazing. I stopped blaming myself and God, and I stopped scaring myself with compulsive, paranoid thoughts about the future. Over time, my free fall into panic and contraction gave way to a wonderful inner feeling of huge expansion.

At the same time, my thinking got clearer and less conventional. I started searching the Internet for accounts of what others with Meniere's disease had done to help themselves heal, and I learned that homeopathy had been very helpful for some. After more research, I started experimenting with several homeopathic remedies from my local health-food store, and, remarkably, one of them began to relieve my symptoms almost immediately!

Oh, the joy of walking again without feeling woozy! And riding a bike and hearing more normally! I could taste the goodness of life again!

Over the following year, I continued to treat myself with homeopathy, and my condition continued to improve until I eventually completely overcame the disease, despite the conventional medical system having told me that couldn't happen.

During this time, my girlfriend broke up with me and, while it was a painful loss, I realized that our relationship hadn't been that healthy for either one of us, anyway. And the love I now felt allowed me to let it go more peacefully, and, happily, that led to my eventually finding and marrying my real soul mate.

So, the illness turned out to hold many profound gifts. The greatest gift of all was that, as it had stripped away my pride and sense of being in control, it had shown me a deeper truth—that the experience of love was the most precious aspect of my life, and it was there underlying everything! The more I opened to love, the more I connected to the unbounded essence that's deeply good and unlimited within us all. I call it Authentic Self-Love, because it's love of who we *truly* are, the Big Self, which is unlimited, not just the mind/bodies we mistakenly *think* we are.

As tough as it was to get through Meniere's disease, these days I'm grateful that I had it. It led to my knowing Authentic Self-Love, which has continued to sustain and transform my life, like sunshine and water sustain a plant. It's not like self-esteem, which comes and goes with circumstances and is a function of the ego that always looks at the outer aspects of life and asks, "How am I doing now?"

Authentic Self-Love is the opposite of that: It *stops* self-judgment and self-doubt. It's on the level of the soul, beyond all the evaluations and comparisons on the surface of life. It always reveals one's essential goodness and wholeness. Whatever your material status in life, whether you're a happily married millionaire or living alone with hardly anything, when you experience Authentic Self-Love, you have an abiding feeling of inspiration, gratitude, wellness, and security.

In my experience, Authentic Self-Love is a warm, accepting embrace that arises from deep within, an inner glow that permeates your entire being. It allows you to "see" the magic within and around you and feel more alive, peaceful, intelligent, and courageous. Your "eyes" are opened by the power of love to see your divine essence, and that transforms your life forever.

By showing you who you really are, Authentic Self-Love also supports the continuous unfoldment of your purpose by revealing the bigger reality you're a part of, and your unique role in it. It allows you to grow toward your full potential and reach for and have all that you need.

And it's a godsend for relationships. In my twenty-three years of practicing psychotherapy I've worked with a lot of unhappy couples, and it's so clear to me now that almost all are suffering (along with most of humanity) from a lack of Authentic Self-Love. The truth is we can't truly love another until we can love ourselves. I've met countless people who are caught in this unhappy predicament, searching for something outside themselves that they have to find inside first.

Another problem caused by the lack of Authentic Self-Love is chronic approval seeking. From childhood, we're conditioned to seek approval and develop strategies to get it, but no amount of approval can ever satisfy our need for love. And even more problems arise when we try to satisfy that need with food, sugar, alcohol, drugs, possessions, and superficial distractions instead. We're merely fooling ourselves, and happiness and peace will continue to elude us.

If you can identify with any of these patterns, take heart! The pain from being run by the fear-based ego can help push you to wake up and become authentically self-loving, free, and secure in yourself. As I learned, suffering ripens us for Authentic Self-Love. And, at any moment, no matter what's happening in your life, Authentic Self-Love can sustain you and transform your life and all your relationships. Because here's the good news: It can show up in our lives during times of crisis, as it did for me, but, thankfully, it can also be cultivated.

If you will devote ten minutes a day to doing what I call Deep Heart Stretches, you will build up your Authentic Self-Love, I promise you. See for yourself how simple yet effective they are.

Five Deep Heart Stretches that Will Wake You up to Authentic Self-Love

1. For two minutes every day: Find the place in your body where you feel most tender, empty, or vulnerable. Notice that there may be an impulse to avoid, numb, fill, cover up, or disconnect from that part. Now imagine yourself like a loving parent holding that part of your body like a baby. If that's difficult, imagine a larger, more loving being like Jesus, the Buddha, or Mother Mary holding that part of you. Imagine warm, kind hands gently soothing you with loving touch. Relax and soften your body. Say these words internally and repeatedly: "I am here, I'm not going away; you are safe; you are precious; I love you." Ask that part to speak to you and, whatever it says, acknowledge the feelings and offer up more love and compassion. Keep reassuring that part that it's okay now to let love in and to let it out, too.

2. For two minutes every day: Breathe love, kindness, and compassion right into your heart. With each inhale, visualize this as multicolored light, descending into and expanding through your chest and gradually filling your whole body. On each exhale, breathe out fear, shame, and self-rejection, visualizing it as a dark smoke or mist. Imagine that smoke or mist dissolving into a clear sky of pure, sparkling light energy. Do this repeatedly while feeling a "thank you" inside.

3. For two minutes every day: Use one of the following verbal activations every day for twenty-one days each, then move on to the next, and the next, until you start again with the first. Say them internally and slowly to yourself, savoring and drinking in the energy that they generate. Say them from what feels like the center of your chest. You can imagine the words creating energetic ripples through your entire body, as though you're dropping pebbles into a pond.

   a. "Like sun rays bursting through clouds, I allow my true self to be revealed by that power greater than my ego. I am learning to see myself through the eyes of Love. Love and I are One and I devote myself to Love! I am grateful and I am growing in the light of Love!"

   b. "I allow my true self to fully shine through the miraculous power of love that's inside of me, starting now. I am a part of the loving intelligence of life and the Universe, which is discovering and celebrating itself uniquely through me. May I deeply embrace all that I am and love my Authentic Self. Thank you."

   c. "I am nothing other than what I truly am, and my real essence is divine and magnificent; what I am is truly enough as I allow myself to fully be; I am lovable in my being and my becoming. And so it is. Thank you."

4. For two minutes every day: Let yourself perceive through the eyes of love. Imagine a living goddess, a great saint, or the most loving human being imaginable. Visualize their face and focus on the eyes and hands. See them looking at you with total love and compassion, with arms and hands outstretched toward you. Feel yourself magnetically drawn to them and slowly opening your heart to receive their love. Now imagine gradually merging with them, so that you are now seeing through their eyes,

looking back at the person that is you. Feel the blessing of being seen as though for the very first time. Relax into the feeling of being seen in that way.

5. For two minutes every day: Be love's body. Imagine that all the cells of your body and all the tissues and organs are made of one primordial, translucent, warm, glowing essence, which is love. Imagine that the fluid of your body is liquid love and that the air you breathe is vaporized love. Imagine that the bones of your body are a solid, structured form of love. Imagine all the cells of your body pulsating and being nourished by the energy of love. Relax into it a little more with every breath, and let yourself feel the love glowing inside you. Repeat silently, "Thank you. I am this."

You can do these deep heart stretches whenever you have a few free moments during the day, or you can do them at a set time all together. Just as your body needs to stretch, so your emotional body also needs to stretch and expand to allow ever more love to move through it. But unlike your body, which can only stretch to its physical limits, I bet you'll discover that the heart can stretch infinitely when given the chance. When you commit to doing these practices every day, you'll see how they'll transform your life and bring you more peace and happiness than ever before!

During the dark night of my healing crisis, I could never have imagined the gifts that were waiting for me on the other side. Wherever you find yourself on your journey and whatever obstacles or challenges you're facing, please trust that Authentic Self-Love is right there for you, too. Because love is your essence—it's the truth of who you really are.

The great Sufi poet Rumi said, "Everything in the universe is within you. Ask all from yourself." And I say, "Ask your self for love and keep asking, and you'll find more than you can imagine."

Sergio Baroni is a licensed psychotherapist, hypnotherapist, and life coach, specializing in helping people experience rapid transformation in their lives. He was a co-developer with Marci Shimoff of the New York Times bestselling book Happy for No Reason. *He was also a co-facilitator of the HeroQuest program, which has helped many people discover their life purpose.*

In his twenty-three years of clinical practice, Sergio has had extraordinary success helping people overcome depression, grief, and addictions; reduce stress and anxiety; and resolve relationship and life-transition issues. He also offers personal intensives on Authentic Self-Love.

Sergio has a private practice in Marin County, California, and can be reached at www.sergiobaroni.com and www.authenticselflove.com.

Chapter 8

Love Is an Inside Job

Melinda Anderson

Your task is not to seek for love but merely to seek and find all the barriers you have built against it.

—Rumi

W here was he?

I was sixteen years old and about to go out on my very first date. Ricky was from a neighboring school and gorgeous and popular. My girlfriend Judy introduced us, and then he called and asked me out. All day long I had been so nervous my palms were sweating as I tried on outfit after outfit, trying to find the right one. I was dressed an hour early and sitting in my room, waiting for him to arrive. But that was an hour and a half ago. *Where was he??*

Ricky never showed up. I didn't leave my room that night. I listened to my 45 of "Maggie May" over and over and over. "You made a first class fool out of me…Maggie, I wished I'd never seen your face." The next day Judy told me she had seen Ricky in town the night before. He told her he didn't go out with me because he had found out I was bald.

It was true. I was born without hair, like some of my relatives. It's a genetic condition. He hadn't known because I wore a wig.

It made me shy as a little child; I used to hide behind my mom's skirts. That feeling didn't go away when I started wearing a wig in the first grade. My classmates all knew I didn't have hair and they acknowledged this new addition with supportive silence. It was never mentioned—at least to my face. But even with the wig, I never felt like I was as good as they were. I played right alongside my friends, but I was constantly on guard that my wig would come off, so I couldn't just relax and have fun. I didn't even want to go outside on a windy day.

On the bright side, I had a wonderful group of friends and a best friend I shared everything with. And things got better in high school. I mostly hung out with the rebel crowd and had sleepover parties with my girlfriends. I wasn't popular or unpopular, just somewhere in between, and from the outside, I looked like a normal kid going through school.

I've wondered since, were my classmates all as unhappy as I was inside? I was full of fear and self-loathing and just tried to be like the others—hoping this would make me be enough. I always wanted to be like someone else because I couldn't believe that anybody would like me the way I was.

As I became an adult, men were drawn to me and I had no problem getting dates; the hard part was enjoying them. I would cringe whenever a man's hands would get close to my neck or face or hair. And then there was always the dreaded moment when I had to tell them about the wig. I feared their rejection even though it never happened. When I finally told them about it and even took it off for them, many men told me I was beautiful with or without it. But I didn't believe them. Without my wig on, I thought I looked like an alien.

Now I can see that some of the men in my life truly were offering me unconditional love; but I couldn't receive it or return it, simply because I couldn't love myself. At the time I was unaware of this, and in my cluelessness, I was a bit of a heartbreaker, dating guys for two years, four years, even six years, and then breaking up with them. Even my marriage to a very dear man couldn't survive my lack of self-love. My former husband was always saddened by my harsh view of myself. He thought I was perfect and beautiful, bare-headed or bewigged.

Little did I know that as long as I looked at my bare head and said, "No one will love you," I was also saying to myself, "I will not love you—or anyone else, either." I didn't know the simple truth that you can't truly love another until you can love yourself.

Over time, I gradually began to accept myself as I was, and, after forty-five years of hiding under a wig, I finally felt freed. I stopped wearing the wig. At the same time I realized that it really doesn't matter if I choose to wear a wig or not: What matters is that I love myself, either way.

So many of us feel inadequate in some way because society has taught us that we have to look or be a certain way in order to be okay. What a difference it made in every part of my life when I stopped believing that and started loving myself just the way I was.

I want to share with you some of the tools I used as I went through the process of self-discovery that I call loving from the inside out.

Loving from the Inside Out
1. Recognize yourself as the source of love
Even if we had a happy, loving childhood, by the time we're teens and interested in the opposite sex, the search for love outside of ourselves

gets kicked into high gear. It's especially easy for girls and women to think we're nothing if we don't have a boyfriend or husband. And how sad is that?

What if we could shift that outward search for love to an inward search? The love we have for ourselves is the foundation of all the love we'll ever be able to feel for anyone else in our lives. If we aren't finding the love we want, we have to start by looking within.

Fortunately, *our essence is love.* In fact, many saints and mystics tell us the whole of creation is nothing but a vibration of love. We are actually "made of love." Of course, that's not always easy to see, in ourselves—or others! But I find that the way we see others is a reflection of the way we see ourselves. If we're judgmental of others, we will be of ourselves too. So we can start to love ourselves more if we can drop some of our judgments of others.

See what happens when you try this exercise called I See No One but Me.

When a person is irritating to you, have the thought, *I see no one but me.* Maybe it's the person at work who bugs you by being needy and taking too much of your time. Look at them and say to yourself silently, "I see no one but me." If you can't see yourself in the person, ask yourself, *Have I ever been needy? Have I ever demanded more attention of someone than they wanted to give?*

We aren't loving ourselves less when we think these thoughts; we're recognizing our human weaknesses and forgiving ourselves, which also allows us to forgive others. We aren't saying that their behavior is okay, only that we see that they are more than their behavior.

So, when someone rudely cuts ahead of you in the supermarket line, think, *I see no one by me.* Not seeing it? Ask yourself, *Have I ever been thoughtless? Can I be selfish when I'm under pressure?*

When we accept the truth that we are all perfectly imperfect and doing the best we can, given our circumstances, our hearts open toward both others and ourselves. We start to see that the ways in which we don't *appear* to be love are just that: *appearances* on the surface and not the truth.

The truth is that love is always there, hidden beneath any action. It's paradoxical, and you may doubt this at first. But practice saying, "I see no one but me," and your heart will soften in love for others, and when that happens, always and equally, your heart will soften in love and acceptance toward yourself, too.

2. Feel your feelings without judgment

One of the greatest things that anyone ever taught me was how to feel. As part of our human experience we are designed to feel. Would you agree that we all have plenty of things to feel? And would you agree that we sometimes turn away from feeling them because it's too uncomfortable? We bury the feeling with food or alcohol or whatever. And guess what? It doesn't go away until we feel it. One day we wake up with a disease and we wonder why.

Learning to feel is different from expressing or acting out emotions. It's detaching the feeling from the mental story connected to the emotion. Those two can feed off of each other, creating an even deeper rut for that emotion. But research shows that a feeling, fully felt, will only last for ninety seconds! Isn't that amazing! Relief is available! But we must drop the mind and be willing to simply feel the feeling. The mind can't heal the emotion, but the heart can.

Here's a practice called Feel the Feeling that I've been using very successfully for about six years:

1. Sit comfortably, uncross your arms and legs, close your eyes, and drop your awareness inside your body.

2. Take three long, slow, deep breaths up the center of your body and focus your awareness on an uncomfortable feeling or emotional sensation. Don't judge it or label it.

3. Without engaging the mind by thinking about any story around it, slowly inhale directly into the sensation. At the top of the breath, say the word *feel* out loud.

4. Slowly exhale, soaking into the sensation, and say out loud, drawing out the word for the whole exhale: *iiiiiiiinnnnn*. We are using the vibration of our voice to meet the energy and feel it, not trying to dissolve or change anything. When we feel it fully, the stuck energy will naturally transmute and, at some point, move freely again.

If you can't go fully into the sensations because they're too uncomfortable, just feel the edge of the sensation, or even the edge of the edge in the beginning. Be gentle with yourself. As you practice over time, see if you aren't taking your feelings as seriously as you used to, and you aren't as afraid to feel them as they arise. They come; they go; life flows on.

3. Practice accepting "what is"

I used to be angry at the unfairness of life. How many other little girls have to worry that their wig will fall off? Now I see it differently. The greater the challenges we have to overcome, the greater the freedom on the other side. So here's my third exercise: Accept "What Is" as a Blessing.

- In every adversity, there's an upside, even if we can't see it at first. Look hard for the upside, and when you find it, give it more of your attention than the downside.
- Whether you can see the upside or not, say, "I accept this as a blessing. It's God's will, and let Thy Will be done."

Most of our suffering comes from our inability, or refusal, to do this. Saints look for and can see the big picture , which is why they don't suffer as we do. But we don't have to be saints to reduce our suffering. We can choose to accept "what is" as a blessing, just as much as we're able to, right now.

When I was a child, I didn't know it was okay, let alone a blessing, to be different, but, fortunately, I learned that over time. And the degree to which I understood and felt that was the degree to which I stopped suffering. As I gradually accepted that being bald didn't mean I wasn't as good as others, I was able to let go of my fear that I could never be loved. And I was finally able to see the beauty that others saw in me.

• • •

As you love yourself more over time, you might find you're more able to let go of things that aren't serving you. Before I could give up my wig, I had been able let go of many things that were hard to part with, including a successful twenty-five-year career for which I had lost my passion, a seven-figure income that was no longer adding value to my life, and a beautiful second home that had outlived its purpose. And most recently, twenty-eight years of breast implants that weren't making me love myself any more. Each time I let something go, it was to accept a truer vision for myself, and so my feelings of love and happiness only grew.

The hardest thing for me to give up was something I thought was love. For many years I was in a relationship that was so hard to leave that we got engaged again after we were divorced! It wasn't working, but I couldn't accept that.

Then, one day, at a metaphysical health fair, I stopped in front of a shaman whose radiance drew me in. A week later, I was in her office, my stomach tied in knots. I tried to blame my recent health challenges on everything other than this relationship. I still wasn't willing to face my fear of being alone again. She listened patiently and then she looked at me with great compassion and said, "You guys are through."

In a torrent of tears, I finally accepted that was the truth. And when the tears ended, I had a taste of freedom. It was time to quit using romantic relationships as Band-Aids and take a new path toward love. I suddenly felt a fierce determination to fill the emptiness inside of me with me! I would no longer depend on another person to make me feel whole. I left my fiancé and devoted myself to my own personal development and eventually to becoming a healer and a teacher.

Today, I'm loving my life as I help people free themselves from their barriers to love. One of the greatest things I've learned is how huge the power of our love is. We are our own lifeline when we discover the greatness of the love inside of us. You can have all the joy and all the love you want in your life. But you have to be willing to take time every day to practice stepping through your barriers to love—even if it's uncomfortable and you feel vulnerable. Even if you have to, metaphorically speaking, take off your wig and show the world your bald head.

Love truly is an inside job. When we start to love ourselves, we discover that it comes pouring in to us from all sides. As the Beatles so beautifully put it, "And in the end, the love you take is equal to the love you make."

Melinda Anderson is a healer, teacher, author, speaker, and certified Passion Test facilitator. Her greatest passion is personal transformation—for herself and others. She aspires to be the change she wishes to see in the world and is committed to helping others become empowered through knowing themselves as the ultimate love.

Melinda has been deeply immersed in her own transformational journey for over fifteen years, which has taken her from a life of self-loathing to a life of self-love. She shares the story of revealing her baldness after forty-five years of hiding under a wig in the women's anthology Speaking Your Truth, Volume II: Courageous Stories from Inspiring Women.

To follow Melinda's journey and advance your own, please visit www.SayYesToYou.com.

Chapter 9

Leaving Self-Doubt Behind: Tap into the Science of Self-Confidence

Louisa Jewell

Years ago I worked as an employment counselor helping women reenter the workforce after many years on social assistance. Most were single mothers barely surviving on a poverty-level government stipend. I wanted them to find jobs that would let them support their families well. Together with a local community college and some funding from the Ontario Women's Directorate, I created a program that gave them not only life skills to succeed in a job but also technical computer skills that were hot in the market. It was the nineties and the Internet had just emerged.

I remember one very bright woman whom I'll call Susan. She became technically savvy so fast that she tutored other women in the program. She picked up new software packages easily and got along with everyone. I was excited when it came time to send out Susan's resume because I knew some employer would snap her up right away.

So you can imagine my shock when Susan flat-out refused to send even *one* resume.

"What's the point?" she said. "Even if I get the job, they'll quickly find out I'm an idiot and fire me."

Wow. My star student had no idea how talented she was. How could someone so obviously capable have such a low view of her own abilities? I was so curious about this behavior that I started on a quest to understand the psychology of self-confidence that enables people to achieve their goals. You see, Susan seemed to be confident about her abilities within the classroom. Whenever she was asked to do something she jumped right in. So what led to her self-sabotage?

Over the last fifteen years, I've discovered that it's not just your knowledge, talent, or skills that drive performance. It's your *beliefs* about your knowledge, talent, and skills. Beliefs drive how people think, behave, and feel. Beliefs affect whether someone perseveres or gives up in the face of obstacles. With self-confident beliefs, people set lofty

Beliefs as Self-fulfilling Prophecies

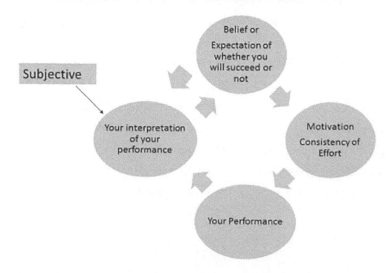

goals and then put in the effort required to succeed. In contrast, self-doubting beliefs lead to procrastination and avoiding opportunities. As Susan demonstrated, many of us hold ourselves back based on doubt in our abilities, even in areas where other people believe we have earned confidence. Sometimes we don't even know why we're doing it.

Beliefs as Self-Fulfilling Prophecies

Let me show you how your beliefs about expected outcomes play a big role in your performance. As an example, let's look at what happens to two friends I've invited to a party.

Sheila, one of the smartest people I know, believes others could not possibly find her interesting because she doesn't have a university degree. Consistent with this belief, she sits at the back of the room chatting with someone she already knows. She never gets up to meet new people. She goes home feeling that since nobody else talked to her, no one must find her interesting. Her belief shapes her behavior, her behavior limits her performance, and her interpretation of her performance reinforces her belief. She made her belief come true.

Now let's look at Denise, who believes she's very engaging and friendly. She makes her way around the room introducing herself, engaging in all kinds of conversations. Because of this experience, she goes home believing she's someone that other people want to know.

If you have a self-doubting belief that you won't succeed, you limit your involvement to protect yourself. Then you aren't surprised when things don't go well. This sends a message back to your brain saying "See, I told you so." The self-doubting belief grows stronger, a self-fulfilling prophecy.

Equally, if you have a positive belief that you can succeed, you engage in behaviors that are likely to lead to success. The outcome sends a message to your brain, "See, I told you that you could do it." Your performance contributes to your confidence, serving as a different sort of self-fulfilling prophecy.

Of course, if Denise went home thinking, "Everyone I spoke to must have thought I was boring as hell," her performance would send a different message to her brain. Even a successful experience could not increase her confidence in the face of self-doubting beliefs.

How can a good performance be undermined by self-doubting beliefs? Denise might compare herself unfavorably to Brenda, who was sociable too and snagged the attention of the hottest guy at the party. Or perhaps Denise spent most of the party walking around with Bernadette, who is equally engaging, so she attributes her success to Bernadette's charm. Do your friends, family, and coworkers keep telling you how amazing you are, but you brush it off saying that you weren't the *real* reason for your success?

I often found it hard to believe my success was due to my talent and skills. So every time I embarked on something new, I always put in a heroic amount of effort because I didn't feel good enough to succeed. I learned years later that this was a symptom of my self-doubt. Gradually, I found ways to overcome that doubt. There isn't space to share my story here, but if you want to know about my journey from self-doubt to self-confidence, watch for my upcoming book: *Beyond Self-Doubt: The New Science of Self-Confidence.*

Three Scientifically Proven Ways to Increase Self-Confidence

So how does one develop self-confident beliefs? Marie Forleo, a popular web video host and successful business coach, once said, "Confidence is overrated. If you wait until you feel confident to start anything, you're never going to start anything." This is especially true when you're embarking on a new venture. Of course you're not going to feel confident in something you've never tried before. So what you need to do is build the kind of confidence that allows you to overcome the fear and do it anyway. When you do things despite your fears, you improve your overall confidence. It becomes an upward spiral. You become better able to meet new challenges, even ones that scare you out of your mind.

Here are three ways to start the upward spiral and keep it going.

Just do it, one step at a time

When Susan would not send out her resumes, I tried to encourage her, but soon I knew there was no way to convince her. So I arranged for her to take a three-month government-paid internship with a local company. At first she was hesitant. "Susan, this company is not paying you a dime, so even if you go there and sweep the floor, they'll be happy you're there. Just do your best." For some reason, this worked, and Susan decided to go.

What I didn't know at the time was that according to science, this is the fastest route to building self-confidence. Psychologists call this a *performance experience*. Perceiving yourself succeed at a certain task and believing that the success is due to your own ability sends a powerful message to your brain: "Yes, I can do it."

When people ask me how to improve self-confidence and I tell them, "Just go do it," they give me funny looks. "Louisa, if I had enough self-confidence, I would have done it a long time ago!" Now the key to building self-confidence using performance experiences is to engage in activities that are highly likely to result in success. If you try something new and fail miserably, it may even increase your self-doubt!

So if you're trying something big, take one baby step toward that goal and think of it as an experiment. Let me give you an example. Perhaps you want to write a book, but the idea scares you because you think, "Who will ever read my book?" or "What if it flops and sells only twelve copies?" Self-doubt around your book might stop you from starting at all.

So try writing an article based on the topic of your book for a local publication. Perhaps you get good comments or people tell you it's great. Then write a few more articles. If that goes well, then you might write a regular blog that comes out monthly. When that goes well, write your blog every two weeks. Some blog postings have more positive comments than others, so you begin to learn what works with your audience. Writing skill comes from practice, so you build your writing capability, getting better and better.

Every successful writing experience leads to an increase in your confidence, which fuels your motivation to work harder and build your skills. If you want to build your self-confidence, rather than focus on the end result, focus on building your capability in small steps. You'll find your self-confidence increases with every successful performance.

If you think of each step as an experiment, you can even learn from setbacks, so that your ability and confidence get better even if you don't always succeed. Perhaps one of your blog postings gets some nasty comments. You look at what people didn't like or found confusing, and you get better at helping them understand. One important ingredient is to care less about what people think and focus more on building your writing skills.

This is exactly how it worked for Susan. She went off to her internship. I heard positive reports from her employer. When Susan returned, I asked her once again, "So Susan, are you ready to send those resumes now?" I was pleasantly surprised with her response.

"Louisa, I sent out a bunch of resumes over a month ago, and I already have a job."

Just three months earlier, there was no budging her. She wouldn't send out even one resume, and now she's already employed!

"Susan, how did you do it?" I asked.

"Louisa, when I got there, I realized I was way better than even half the people that worked there!" She had to *experience* it before she would believe it. Susan had some deeply held beliefs that she was worthless, stemming from childhood abuse. If Susan can overcome entrenched self-doubts, so can you.

Seek positive encouragement

Some people require powerful words of encouragement to move forward. This is another contributing factor for self-confidence that psychologists call *social persuasion.*

When you decide to embark on something new, you may find that the naysayers show up. People tell you, "You can't do that!" or "Gosh, are you sure you have it in you?" I heard comments like these even from good friends. They undermined my motivation to move toward my dreams. I felt as if someone were bursting my balloon just as it was rising toward the sky.

On the other hand, someone who constantly encourages you can be a catalyst for achievement. The right word, said at the right time, can give you the energy to move on.

Social persuasion should not be underestimated. Neuroscientists have discovered that we are much more socially hard-wired than we knew before. Very deep within us, we want to be accepted. We want to fit in. If you fear doing something that will garner social criticism, your brain goes on high alert with the fear that reaching for your big dream might threaten your social standing.

If you want to build your self-confidence in a certain area, you have to learn how to ignore the naysayers and surround yourself with people who believe in you and your cause. This is why coaches can be so effective. Sports coaches, wellness coaches, career coaches, and writing coaches are paid to be on your side and help you succeed.

Find powerful role models

As social creatures, we turn to others around us to learn appropriate behavior. As children, we learn by watching our parents, teachers, and siblings. We behave in similar ways to our friends. This is why role models are so important for building self-confidence. If you never see a female airline pilot, you might believe that it's not possible for women to become pilots. Or you might think that becoming an airline pilot might reflect poorly on you as a woman and hurt your future social desirability.

Science has shown that modeling is more effective when the role model is similar to you. For example, if I'm a twenty-five-year-old woman, I'm more likely to believe I can run a marathon too if I see another young woman running one than if I see a young man. One fascinating research study showed that the gap in standardized test scores between African American and other students disappeared after Barack Obama became president. This one study suggests that role models contribute to changing beliefs and fueling greater self-confidence.

If you don't have any role models doing what you want to do, use LinkedIn to find some. Join networking groups they are likely to attend. Ask your friends or parents for ideas. Interview potential role models, take them for coffee, or have a good email exchange. Learning how they succeeded will increase your belief that you can do it too. Don't be afraid to ask. People who would be good role models often find it highly rewarding to contribute to another's success.

For years I was about ten pounds heavier than I wanted to be. I thought that was the way I was, so I ate and exercised accordingly. Then I saw my friend Sabrina had become slim and toned. I asked her how she got in such phenomenal shape. She told me she did hot yoga every day and ate a vegan diet. By seeing her, I realized for the first time that I could do it too. I said to myself, "Why not me?" So I started doing hot yoga every day and eating differently and soon I started to lose weight too. Sabrina was a powerful role model for me.

Susan's Success

In Susan's case, she had all three elements working together to help her shift her beliefs. Her internship offered her an opportunity to have performance experiences. I paired her with a mentor her own age who acted not only as a role model, but also gave her social persuasion in the form of encouraging words in the face of setbacks. Once Susan's beliefs shifted, she was self-confident enough to send out her resume.

Now apply this in your life. What is that dream that you never believed you could reach? Set mini goals and start building self-confidence step by step. Surround yourself with competent and encouraging people. Seek out and get to know people like you who have already achieved this dream. *Believe* that it is possible. Start now…Your dreams are waiting!

Louisa Jewell is a speaker, author, facilitator, and positive psychology expert who has inspired thousands of people around the world to flourish with confidence both at work and in their personal lives. Louisa founded the Canadian Positive Psychology Association and is a graduate of the Master of Applied Positive Psychology program at the University of Pennsylvania, led by renowned psychologist Dr. Martin Seligman. Her work has been featured in Forbes, The Globe and Mail, Huffington Post, Live Happy *magazine,* Chatelaine, Psychology Today, Women's Agenda, *and many more.*

For more tips on how to flourish with confidence, visit www.louisajewell.com.

Chapter 10

Prepare for Take-Off:
Release Your Fears and Soar

Maggie Dillon Katz

N o one knew.

Not my husband. Not my mother. Not my best friend. No one knew the fear I'd been hiding for ten years.

It first gripped me when I was eight years old, standing on the hot tarmac at JFK airport. The Air Canada plane towered over my mother, my ten-year-old brother, and me as we said good-bye. I was anxious and upset. I didn't want to leave my mother, so I didn't want to get on that plane, even though I'd been looking forward to seeing my cousins in Canada.

The stewardess beckoned to us; it was time to say goodbye. My stomach lurched. I gave my mother a hug and kiss. Then I climbed the steps, hot tears spilling down my cheeks. At the top, I looked back at my mother, shielding my eyes to hide my tears. I forced a smile, waved, and, as I turned and stepped into the plane, anxiety overwhelmed me.

I felt like I was heading off to another galaxy. I was afraid I'd never see my mother again.

And so, my uneasy relationship with flying and being separated from loved ones was born. Fast forward to 2002, one year after 9/11. I hadn't flown in nine years, since a scare on a flight while I was in the Peace Corps in the Marshall Islands, just before I'd become pregnant with our daughter. And since 9/11, the fear was worse, as I'd been having nightmares of going down in plane crashes. I missed traveling to faraway places and having exotic adventures, but I couldn't get past my fear. I was too embarrassed to speak about it to anyone, so I was hiding it—and keeping my life small.

As our daughter grew older, my husband sometimes suggested we fly to places we'd never been. I knew what to say to end the discussion: "No, let's save our money." He'd happily agree, pleased that I was being the budget-conscious one for a change.

Then I applied for a job with a program to support young adults with learning differences. The interview was going well, and it all sounded great until the director said the job would involve a few trips a year—and I'd have to fly.

"You'd be away three to five days. Would that work for you?" he asked. He knew I had an eight-year-old. I felt queasy. Fly and leave my daughter at the same time?

"Uhh…yes," I said. "That could work." But I wondered, *Could it?*

I got the job, and I was thrilled. It was work I loved that accommodated my daughter's school schedule and gave me summer's off. Perfect! Except I had to fly.

I bought a book: *The Anxiety and Phobia Workbook: A Step-By-Step Program for Curing Yourself of Extreme Anxiety, Panic Attacks, and Phobias,* by Edmund Bourne, PhD. I liked the dedication, "…to anyone who has struggled with anxiety or an incomprehensible fear." I studied the chapter on visualization. I was wildly imaginative and saw life in pictures, so this was ideal for me. I read, "You may or may not be able to will your way to a particular goal, yet repeatedly visualizing the attainment of that goal has a good chance of bringing exactly what you seek." There was hope!

I followed the guidelines and practiced imagining myself driving to the airport, walking through security, sitting in the waiting area, stepping into the plane, and walking to my seat. During my practice sessions, my heart raced, my palms got sweaty, and my mouth went dry. But with more practice I made shifts and my anxiety began to lessen. I thought I could do it. I *had* to do it!

But the week of the flight I couldn't sleep. Nightmares of crashes continued to haunt me. I needed more visualization practice!

The day of my flight arrived. I was filled with anxiety but made it to my seat. I was shaky as I waited for takeoff, but the plane didn't move. We waited and waited.

Something was wrong.

Finally, the captain's voice came over the speakers. "Ladies and gentlemen, this is your captain. I'm sorry for the delay, but we have a little part we need to repair."

No! No! This can't be happening, I thought. *Please God, no! Why did he have to tell us this? I do not want to know about broken parts!*

He came on again. "Ladies and gentlemen, this is your captain again. We've decided we are not going to fix the part. So we'll be pushing off soon."

"Oh, my God," I said. That sounded worse. My heart raced and I started to sweat.

Five minutes passed. He came on again, "Ladies and gentlemen, we've decided we are going to fix the part. I apologize for the further delay."

I took a deep breath of relief. "Phew!" My nerves were jangled.

Another five minutes passed, then, "Ladies and gentlemen, we've decided we won't fix the part. It's the starter motor. We will be fine."

The starter motor?! That didn't sound like something you could do without! Fear rose like a tidal wave, filling my gut and chest. I saw the whole scene in an instant: We were crashing, screaming, on the verge of death! I began an internal dialogue:

I've got to get off this plane!

No, you can do it. Stay on the plane!

No. I can't.

I snapped. I tore at the seat belt, jumped up, and walked quickly up the long aisle to the front of the plane.

I felt 250 pairs of eyes boring into my back. I didn't care. I was getting off. I'd never see them again. I reached the front, startling the two male flight attendants, who jumped in their small fold-down seats. They looked up, wide-eyed.

"Ma'am, we've closed the door. You must go back to your seat," one said.

"No, I want to get off the plane." My voice was soft yet determined.

"Ma'am, the door is shut! You must sit down."

"I want to get off." I repeated quietly. We had a short standoff. I didn't move. Then he reached up, pulled down the phone receiver, and said, "Captain, we have a woman who wants to get off the plane." Pause. Then he handed me the phone.

"Hello?" I said in a small voice.

"Hello." The pilot had a warm voice, rich as honeyed mahogany. "What is your name?"

"Maggie Katz."

"Well, Maggie," he said, "tell me. What's the problem?"

"I, I want to get off the plane."

"And why is that?"

"I don't feel safe."

"Let me tell you something, Maggie. First, I am the father of three teenage sons, and I have a wife I love very much. I would never do anything that would compromise my making it home. Equally important, Maggie, I would never, ever, do anything that would put my passengers in danger.

"Oh," I said.

"Lastly," he said, "the starter motor. It sounds important, but it's not."

"Oh," I said.

"We don't need it to take off, fly, or land," he said. "It's like if the CD player in your car broke. You can still drive the car."

"Oh." I felt calmer.

"So, Maggie, what do you think? Do you think you can fly?"

"Yes."

"Are you sure?"

"Yes. I'm sure." I knew I could.

"Okay, that's great."

"Thank you so much." My voice wobbled; my eyes filled with tears.

"You're welcome." And his warm voice clicked off.

Flushed with embarrassment, I turned and faced the passengers, all 250 of them, then, keeping my eyes downcast, made my way back to my seat.

"Sorry," I whispered to the man sitting beside me. I buckled up and looked out at the tarmac to hide my mortification. But I felt calmer.

The captain came over the speakers. "Ladies and Gentlemen, I want to share something with you…"

He went on to tell them what he'd told me about the starter motor and how it wasn't needed to fly. I felt a collective whoosh of many sighs of relief. Shoulders and bellies relaxed and the tension left the plane. I felt less foolish.

The flight was smooth. We landed safely. I waited to be the last passenger to get off the plane so I could thank the pilot. I walked up the aisle beaming like a bride, and when I saw him we each broke into a broad smile.

"Maggie?" he asked.

"Yes." I nodded.

"How was it?"

"Good. Thanks to you, I was fine! Thank you so much for your kindness!"

I stepped off the plane, wanting to do a victory dance. I had made it. I was bigger than my fear! Even if it was there, I could move through it.

My life opened up once again. Adventure beckoned.

• • •

Do you have a secret, paralyzing fear you wish you could get beyond? I didn't completely get over my fear that day, but through visualizations, sensory practices, writing, and cognitive exercises, my capacity to face my fear has continued to grow. I still don't love to fly. But I accept it as part of a richer life, one that has included the opportunity to live in New Zealand and visit my daughter when she studied abroad in Copenhagen.

Have you ever had an experience, like mine, where two anxieties merged into a visceral fear? Tackling my fear of flying and the emotions of separation and loss it raised became an opportunity for me to learn how to stay connected to myself and loved ones, while letting go of fear and anxiety. For years I was ashamed of my fear of flying until I realized that fear has a purpose and could be my teacher.

"What?" you say. "Fear can be my teacher?"

Ask yourself: *Is my fear a genuine warning sign of real danger? Or is my fear keeping me from taking a healthy risk?* Both kinds of fear feel the same in your body. But the second kind keeps you small and prevents you from taking risks that could enrich and expand your life. The trick is to know one from the other!

Here are five steps you can take to learn when to trust your gut and how to turn fear from a prison guard into a life teacher.

Step 1: Take Baby Steps to Let It Go

It's helpful to realize that you don't have to let your fear go all at once. You can begin with baby steps. There's an African proverb that says, "Smooth seas do not make skillful sailors," and that sounds true to me, but it's good to *begin* your practice in smooth seas and slowly build your capacity to handle rougher emotional seas through cognitive, visual, and sensory practices that will support you. The process is similar to the work of building muscles and getting fit over time.

Step 2: Turn Fear into Your Teacher

Befriend your fear so it can advise you. If you allow it to have a voice, rather than stuffing it down and letting it hijack your emotions and body, you'll give it an opportunity to become your teacher. So, let your fear express itself. Do your best to listen, acknowledge, and respond to its concerns.

Let's start now while you're calm. Get a notebook or journal and write your answers to the following questions without judging yourself. Research has shown that journaling about your fears reduces them.

1. What is the fear or anxiety you want to release?
2. Why do you want to get beyond the fear?
3. What are you yearning for? What is the outcome you'd like to have, beyond the fear?
4. What would you do or be if you didn't have this fear?
5. What is the value of this fear or anxiety? How does it keep you safe?
6. What does the fear want you to know? What does it want you to do?

7. What does your heart want you to do? What does your inner guidance, or higher source of guidance, want you to do?

Step 3: Thank Your Fear for Keeping You Safe

If your answers lead you to realize that your fear or anxiety has been keeping you from pursuing a larger dream out of a desire to keep you safe, thank it for protecting you for all these years. You can reduce your fear by no longer being afraid of it but accepting it as a force that is on your side. Let it know you appreciate its love and care for you, and tell it that it can let go now because you're taking steps to feel safe and be safe, so you no longer need its help.

Step 4: Visualize Your Successful Outcome

You can begin with the end in mind with this exercise. Find a quiet, comfortable spot where you won't be disturbed and you can relax. You can do this lying down or sitting.

1. Close your eyes and dream about what you want to achieve beyond the fear and anxiety.
2. Visualize the perfect outcome of this dream in your life.
3. Take in four slow, deep breaths, relaxing your body more and more as you inhale and exhale.
4. Imagine yourself in a place you love that brings you a sense of tranquility. Continue to take deep breaths as you feel yourself relax into this place of rest.
5. Now, imagine you've just walked through the fire of your fear and come out the other side. It's done. You've succeeded!
6. What do you see? Where are you? What is the setting? Inside? Outside? What is the atmosphere like around you? Is anyone with you? What are they saying to you?

7. What are the smells, sounds, colors, and feelings or energies around you?

8. What are you thinking and feeling? What is your heart, head, gut, or intuition telling you? Where in your body do you feel this?

9. Imagine yourself celebrating your accomplishment. Is anyone celebrating it with you?

Step 5: Savor Your Accomplishment

Hold these images and feelings of success in your heart and mind for five to ten minutes. We know from research on the brain that positive visualizations build new neural pathways in your brain to help you create the reality. Come back to these images and practice this final step frequently.

Eleanor Roosevelt once said, "You gain strength, courage, and confidence by every experience in which you really stop to look fear in the face…You must do the thing you think you cannot do." When you can do that thing you think you cannot do, your life will take off and you will soar!

Maggie Dillon Katz is a contributing author to the Amazon bestseller Breakthrough! Inspirational Strategies for an Audaciously Authentic Life. *A passionate speaker, Maggie leads transformational workshops supporting parents and their young adult on staying connected while letting go, releasing anxiety and overgiving, and embracing the gifts of hypersensitivity.*

Maggie inspires women to love themselves, claim their gifts, and find their voice to serve themselves and the world. She walks the path she teaches and brings humility and humor to the work and stories she shares.

She has a daughter in college and lives with her husband in the Berkshire Mountains in Massachusetts.

Please connect with Maggie and www.maggiedillonkatz.com.

Chapter 11

Basta Ya! Enough Already! Grandma Shaman's Advice for Living a Kick-Ass Life

Mayra Fernandez

I am your Grandma Shaman.

Shamans are wise elders sent to help others gain universal wisdom. It is a calling: to live a life of purpose by sharing wisdom and happiness. I tell stories laced with ancient principles to benefit those who want to live a kick-ass life, where dreams are renewed every day as they float from one's heart and are transformed into action to create a life of one's choosing.

My fervent hope, dear heart, is that, upon reading these pages, you and those you love will be spared the misery that many of us have suffered, and that, if suffering should come, the words "*Basta ya!* Enough already!" are always on hand for your own deliverance.

I know you already. You think we've never met, *cariño*, but you just don't remember quite as deeply as I do. Knowing you, I can safely say, "I love you." Why? Because I'm your Grandma Shaman! And I know you most definitely want to live a kick-ass life. Why? Because *basta ya!* Enough already!

Here is my story. Read it with your eyes and your heart.

Especially your heart.

• • •

"You can't do this!" my therapist screeched. "I'll lose my license!"

"Don't worry," I calmly replied. "My suicide note will say you had nothing to do with my killing myself."

"But you're Catholic!" Her screech had become a wail. "It's against your religion! You'll go to hell!"

"God will understand," I responded, and, ever so slowly, I enunciated the next words clearly and precisely. "*This* is hell."

With surprising coldness, I had telephoned my therapist to inform her of my imminent suicide. She had tried so hard to help me. I had wanted to say thank you and goodbye.

It was the Wednesday before Thanksgiving. Two years previously, I had had my twelve children, six of whom were adopted, and thirty-two guests in my home for my usual sit-down dinner. Those were good times. But now I had only my two youngest for Thanksgiving because, since those days, I had discovered my sexual identity as a lesbian, divorced the man everybody—myself included—had long assumed was the perfect husband, and lost all but my littlest ones.

I had spent decades wondering why deep happiness had skipped my doorstep. After all, I did have the "perfect" husband: a churchgoer, a nonsmoker, nonalcoholic, hardworking professional who made a good income, helped with the kids, and didn't womanize. How could I possibly complain? So I didn't. Can you picture it, *mi cielo?*

But living with my husband had been torture. I had been living a lie that I could no longer maintain and it was suffocating me.

Are you with me, mi vida?

I hadn't wanted to break up the family. Instead, I proposed a possible solution to my husband: separate bedrooms. "Your body is mine!" was his response. His physical response wasn't lovely either.

Little by little with the help of family and friends I had brainwashed myself into thinking that I was happy. He had brainwashed me too in believing that I was the lucky one to have such a "perfect" husband. There was no protesting on my part, and that, *cariño*, is the classic scenario of abuse. You are told you are at fault. And you believe it!

I had done everything I could to make my husband and children happy, yet it all came tumbling down with my one decision to live with integrity, finally admitting to myself and my loved ones who I was. I wanted to own the pink slip for my life, to be able to say when enough was enough and get out of that abusive marriage.

But this new life was worse.

Being ostracized, not allowed to see my older children, was indeed hell. Because I had dared to choose happiness instead of living a life of lies about who I was, I found myself in a forced exile from my nine adolescent children, my church, and my extended family and friends. Mom forbade family members from relating to me. My teens, according to their father, wanted nothing to do with me. Several times, when I asked for the court-appointed weekends, he screamed, veins popping, "The children don't love you!" I believed him! And, most heartbreaking, I believed my little ones would be happier to be back with the rest of the family, instead of lonely and isolated with me.

My solution? A lethal dosage of pills. Instead of finding happiness, I had become a victim, and victimhood had opened the door to depression and an attitude of worthlessness. I hung up the phone, sat down with the bottle of pills in my left hand, a scratchy pen in my right, and lucidly began my suicide note, as I popped one pill at a time.

It was my dark night of the soul. At that time there was no 911 to call. I wrote my letter because I just wanted somebody, anybody, to understand, and I slowly swallowed pills. Each pill represented a family member or friend who had abandoned me, including my autocratic mother. God, who had once been my best friend, was so distant, it didn't seem I could reach Him. But, after the tenth, or maybe it was the fourteenth, pill my thoughts began to slowly shift with each swallow. *How did I get to this point in my life where dark beliefs and actions were threatening my very existence? When had I allowed the false ideas imposed by my ex-husband, mother, church, and society to become a part of my belief system? What had happened to the strong, vibrant, ambitious, already-published, award-winning eighteen-year-old school president who was going to set the world on fire?*

That dark night I paused in my pill-popping drama and stopped to imagine my teen children loving and respecting me once more and my two youngest thriving and happy. I imagined myself feeling the joy of being alive again, receiving the doctoral degree I had long wanted, and holding my published books in my hands.

I put down the pill bottle. The moment I changed my attitude and chose to see my life as valuable, I stopped taking the pills.

In the coming days, I woke up to life again. I did research and talked to women from many professions, ages, religions, and cultures, straight women and lesbians, who, like me, had been in crisis and decided *basta ya! Enough already!* I found that we all had followed basic universal principles that had resulted in action and a life fully lived. A kick-ass life! For the blossoming of your precious life, *querida*, I want to briefly share these seven universal principles with you now.

1. Choose Happiness

Yes, we have to *choose* to be happy. It is an *unalienable right*, one I strongly believe to be codified in our DNA—but only if you claim it! It might be difficult at first, but, as many shamans have said, you do have to put out some effort if you want to lead a kick-ass life, dearest.

In her own pursuit of happiness, Marci Shimoff, author of the *New York Times* bestseller *Happy for No Reason,* found that those who really put their minds to being happy do, indeed, end up being "happy for no reason" and living a kick-ass life.

I decided I was worthy of happiness, even in this forced exile, the worst situation I could imagine. Still, it was up to me to find it just as it's up to you—which brings me to the second important principle I want to share with you, *amorcito.*

2. Attitude Is Everything

Choose an attitude adjustment, sweet child of my heart. For me, it had to be one worthy of the passions I had deep within me. According to science, a dark hole in space is where old stars go to die and new ones are born. In my dark night of the soul I let my fears and expectations die and my dreams bear fruit.

Then, *mi hija,* I matched my "I can" with an "I will!" Choosing to change my attitude took a degree of courage I thought I didn't have. But I discovered my courage had always been there, potentially. Just as yours is. You just need to call it by name. Your name. Your courage has your name on it, just as mine has my name, brave heart. There is no monopoly here.

Next I decided to do a courageous thing to liberate *myself.*

3. To Be Free, Forgive

All major belief systems stand on this universal principle: Forgive those who hurt you. It takes courage to forgive, not the greeting-card sentimentality kind of forgiveness, but forgiveness with ovaries! Yes, *ovarios*! And ovaries we've got! So next I decided to do the most courageous thing of all: Forgive everyone who was shunning me or had hurt me, including my ex-husband and my mother.

This is a journey that does not often come easy, *querida*. It didn't for me. When I lost my adolescent children and my extended family, I also lost my home, my volunteer church work, my "groupies," and my standing in the community. All I had left was my integrity, my two little boys, and my teaching job, the last two I was very fearful of losing to my homophobic society.

So, I know you hear me, dear one, when I tell you these fears and losses made forgiving not easy for me! Just as I know they will not be easy for you, but you'll discover that forgiveness is the only path to happiness. It comes down to a choice: Would I rather be right or would I rather be happy? When you choose happiness, forgiveness is a requirement.

And there was more, *mi reina*! Forgiveness leaves a giant hole in the heart. Abhorring a vacuum, Nature immediately fills this hole with the most exquisite elixir in the universe: love. Drink of it.

4. Love

This is *the* most universal of principles: Love follows forgiveness. When my heart softened in forgiveness, love was there. And with love flowing, joy came back into my life. Regardless of what others felt, if I could feel love, I could be happy. My life looked the same outwardly, but it was transformed, simply because I bore more goodwill to everyone in my world. And that was obviously enough to rebuild my life just like it will be for you. From love, even more joy came when I began to imagine what that new life would be like.

5. Imagination Inspires Us

During that dark night I paused and pictured my two youngest as responsible, happy adults and my teens as loving peers who respected me again. I imagined me all smiles, graduating with a doctoral degree and caressing my name on the covers of my published books. I saw myself finally free to be me.

Imagine your new life, too, free to have and be whatever you desire. Who will you be? What will you do? Who will you spend your time with? You have the power to design the life you wish to live. Now is the time to picture it.

So get a notebook or a journal and start writing. What will your ideal life look like? What will it feel like? If you're artistic, draw pictures of that life. If you express yourself best in words, then record your description of that life. Make it part of yourself. This is the first step of making it real, dear one.

Once I got clear, I took a stand for my beliefs and fought for them. I found allies to support me in my fight, just like you will. This led me to understand the next principle.

6. It Takes a Village to Grow a Person

When an astronaut was asked, "What was the most important lesson learned from the space program?" she quickly replied, "One cannot do it alone. It takes a team." I subsequently created a new team composed of my chosen family, one not tied by blood or surname, but a truly supportive system. Those were my courageous action steps to honor who I am, the one God made in Her image and I was made whole again, *mi hija.*

Who will you invite onto your team? Who will be your village? In your journal, begin writing out the names of the people in your world whom you know you can trust, who will be there for you no matter what. You're designing the life you were meant to live. Who will share it with you?

The final step made everything real for me.

7. Choose Faith over Fear

I had been a woman absorbed in fear: fear of being outed and therefore losing my job, fear of my little ones being taken from me as my ex-husband constantly threatened, fear of losing my grip on life. Faith and fear are similar, both often being *a belief in something that* appears *not to be happening.* That night and subsequent days and nights after that, I chose faith over fear.

The words of mystic Julian of Norwich speak directly to my experience that Wednesday night. Perhaps they speak to yours as well? "God did not say, 'You won't have storms, you won't have struggles, you will not be dis-eased,' but God did say, 'You will not be overcome.'" I was not overcome. I overcame, *querida*! You can overcome, too! *Sí*!

Visionary Mary Morrissey would later tell me, "Your fear is not bigger than your God." I now ask you: Faith and life? Or fear and death? You have a choice. *L'chaim*! To life!

I know how far south abuse can take someone, but I also know that the wisdom of the North, my God, did not abandon me. Whatever form that creative power that has birthed this experience called life takes for you, know that you will never be alone.

Today I celebrate my life and the ways in which, through my experiences, I can help others, dear, sweet woman. This is the purpose behind our pain and suffering. You and I, we have learned the hard way. Now is our chance to help others avoid the misery we fell into.

That Thanksgiving Eve would be the last time I thought my life so worthless that I would attempt to end it. At the time I could not fathom the Buddha's words: "When you realize how perfect everything is, you will tilt your head back and laugh at the sky." It took me a while. First, in my depression I had to acknowledge that there was a sky. And next, that I would be able to laugh again someday. Just as you will!

Today I laugh! And why? Because I live a kick-ass life! Why? Because *basta ya!* Enough already!!

Born in the Dominican Republic, *Dr. Mayra Fernández,* known as Grandma Shaman, is the author of eighteen books, a public speaker, a visionary, and the proud mother of seventeen children, eleven of them adopted. An award-winning teacher with a doctorate in multicultural education from the University of San Francisco, Mayra has lived in six different countries and has traveled the world, garnering knowledge and wisdom to share with you.

At the websites below, you can request a free download of the Seven Universal Principles, order the book Basta Ya! Enough Already!, view the blog, or contact Grandma Shaman to find out more about her presentations, books, seminars, and videos in English or Spanish. Visit www.bastayaenoughalready.com and www.grandmashaman.com.

Chapter 12

Pilgrim in Prada: How to Live a First-Class Life and Liberate Your Soul

Anita Catalano

The privilege of a lifetime is to become who you truly are.
—**Joseph Campbell**

The piercing blast of the alarm sounded like a foghorn in the dead of night. Another Groundhog Day lay ahead—one like all the days before. Relentless.

I rolled over and stared across the vast expanse of our new king-size bed. My husband lay sleeping, oblivious to the fate that awaited us. I'd long forgotten that familiar smell when you've loved someone for years—that unique and soothing scent that comes with long, loving partnerships. Now it felt like the Great Wall of China divided us.

After mulling over countless exit strategies, today, I was going to tell him our marriage was over. The marriage my friends and family thought was made in heaven, the marriage that people thought would never fail, the partnership that seemed to have it all.

To the outside world I did have it all. I'd married well. My husband was the grandson of a famous Australian. We lived in a fancy house, drove nice cars, and had a nanny. I enjoyed weekly beauty treatments, designer clothes, and overseas holidays. Thrown into the desirable mix was a great career as a journalist and a well-paid job in the corporate world.

But at home in our nest—where it really mattered—life was a different story. We didn't argue, but we didn't talk either. Don't get me wrong, my former husband is a fantastic dad and a good man, but, sadly, we'd become like passing ships in the night.

As our eighteen-year union trudged along, my husband and I had become like chalk and cheese, incompatible with not a lot in common anymore. There were no torrid affairs or sexual pursuits on either side. Put simply, we'd drifted apart with no modern-day GPS to navigate our way back to each other.

Like so many, our lives had become busier than a blender at breakfast. Between yoga classes, dates for coffee, and never-ending family, work, and social obligations, life rolled on without pause. And I needed to take a pause. I'd realized it's not until we reach our forties that many of us put on the brakes and discover there's a nagging void that needs nurturing. For some this void is a crisis; for others it creates a space for a wonderful awakening.

So on a scorching summer day in Sydney, I turned my world upside down, taking many in its wake. I had to flourish again, to discover what made me tick. I needed to find my truth—and fast.

You see, I'd always been the "yes" girl—overcommitting to people, events, and daily tasks. I started off pleasing my parents, then my boyfriends, my husband, and children. I wanted everyone to be happy—at my own expense. Speaking my truth in relationships was like drawing blood from a stone. Along the way I not only lost my voice but also myself.

Can you relate? If so, this chapter was written for you.

Maybe, like me, you've asked yourself if you can find yourself without having to retreat to a mountain top for months of silent meditation or giving away your worldly possessions. After my divorce, I was ready for a spiritual journey, but I wanted to do it in my own way—my own style—and in my favorite high heels.

My pilgrimage began in Sedona, Arizona, one of the world's spiritual hubs. I packed a suitcase, hugged my children, and prepared myself for seven days of intensive healing sessions that would see me whispering to horses, pacing around medicine wheels in the desert, and crossing over to the other side.

Sedona changed everything. I met God in Sedona—I'm positive I did.

My adult years were plagued with doubts whether God really existed, and I still don't consider myself religious, but something profound took place on a hot June day a few years back.

Anahata was my final session for the day. A transformational and shamanic healer, Anahata had trained with the great spiritual masters in Peru, Asia, India, and North America. I was in good hands.

Yet the last thing I wanted to do was sit around and bang on some drums. My jeans were soaked with sweat from the desert heat and my brain was mush. Earlier that day, Shaman Joseph White Wolf had interpreted a dream he had about me, and in another session I rehashed unhappy memories with a woman who had worked with the Dalai Lama. I was done with all this midlife mayhem. Finding myself was becoming too hard.

Couldn't I just skip this final session? *No one will know*, I thought to myself. I walked up the path to Anahata's home. Wind chimes still in the stifling heat. I knocked hard on the door, grazing my knuckles. A petite woman with long blonde tresses and an angelic face slowly opened the door, gracefully welcoming me into her home. Wow, this woman oozed peace. Anahata looked like she'd be more at home riding the waves at a California beach than helping me unlock my demons.

We sat down together in the coolness of her living room to talk about what would happen over the next hour. She said at one point during the session she would ask me to hold my breath.

"I have asthma," I said.

"Don't worry. You will be OK, but assure me you'll come back to the room," she said. I nodded and thought, *Of course I'm coming back. I'm not going anywhere.*

That was the cue for the session to begin. Loud music bellowed around the room while Anahata beat her African drum, chanting and telling me to breathe faster and faster. I soon found myself flying headfirst down a long dark tunnel. I could hear the music beating throughout the room, but only just. As I sped down the dark passage my throat started to tighten and I could feel tears streaming down my face. Anahata gently tapped my throat to clear the blockage, and then asked me to hold my breath. I was flung from the darkness. If there was a heaven on earth, this was it. Water cascaded down the cliff glittering like diamonds; lush leaves in the forest sparkled like emeralds. I could hear the sweet sound of birds, see tiny butterflies in every color of the rainbow, and smell the lusciousness of the rainforest.

Just above the top of the waterfall I saw the face of a man; his eyes looked straight into mine. If this was Jesus I was staring right at him. I didn't want to breathe and spoil this crazy sense of peace and euphoria that washed over me. I wanted to stay right here with him and feel like this forever.

"You cannot stay here, you must go back," he said. I didn't question why but I didn't want to go back either. I trusted him. I began to breathe again, flying back through the darkness flanked by loved ones who had passed. I don't know who they were but I could feel them on either side. As I opened my eyes in Anahata's living room I sobbed—

releasing a mixture of fear and excitement and knowing that I might have just met Jesus.

Now that I had found God's love, I needed to find love here on earth. Could a forty-something woman be so lucky? I briefly dabbled in online dating without success: Gary had been married for twenty-five years, was bored, and wanted some fun on the side; Martin squeezed my hands a little too hard; and Paul's wife had just left him for a woman.

Then lust struck playing Words with Friends, an online version of Scrabble. "RedDevil" lived halfway across the world in America and was a whiz with words. This man had a brain. Check. He could construct a decent sentence. Check. He was well read. Triple-check! Online chats progressed to phone calls, Skype, then love…or so we thought.

We'd planned to make our online love affair real in New York—in the dead of winter. In our heads we were already living happily ever after.

But after much hype, our first and brief union was a disaster—on an apocalyptic scale. Not that he was ugly; he was shorter than I imagined and had a smile that revealed teeth a color that made my stomach churn.

I felt like I'd walked straight onto the set of *50 Shades of Grey*. I soon discovered he was into playing games with blindfolds and leather belts, while I just wanted to cuddle. He wanted to tie me up, and I just needed to talk. At fifty-two, he was still bitter about his divorce ten years ago and trying to find his niche in life. After two miserable days together, I realized finding love again at my age was going to be more difficult than climbing Mt. Everest. I was an intelligent, sane woman, so how did I end up of the other side of the world with a strange man in my room? The pursuit of love makes you do weird things. And things did get weirder.

How could an intelligent, sensible woman be so careless? My friends and family thought I'd died and gone to shake hands with the devil.

When you reach midlife you start to realize that your childhood dreams of immortality and specialness have been a fantasy. Essentially, this is what a midlife crisis forces you to confront: the harsh realities of adult life.

Many of us are raised to put other people's needs before our own. We grow up assuming that if we follow the rules everything will work out and we'll live happily ever after. But when you reach the halfway mark, you realize life is not that simple.

My sacred yet stylish pilgrimage is still a work in progress. However, I have found a simple way to live a first-class life with a liberated soul. Freedom found.

My ex-husband and I are slowly creating new lives and picking up the pieces that go hand-in-hand with divorce. To this day, he doesn't understand my journey or need to fill that void, but we've reached a polite and respectful space that shows our children divorce doesn't have to suck. Having found that even the torment the Universe has given me is something to be thankful for since it forced me to take a new direction, I have found purpose, direction, strength, adventure...and a new love in my life.

Have I given up the nice car, stopped buying stylish clothes, downsized my house, or cut off all my hair? No, I haven't. I'm living proof you can still find your authentic self in your favorite dress and heels!

Here are six steps to create a more authentic, liberated life—on your terms.

1. Be Real

When you aren't living a life that's true for you, you'll notice a nagging void in your soul—something missing you can't put your finger on. The concept of being "authentic" gets tossed around a lot, but it really means coming from a place within. It is being yourself, not an imitation of what you or others think you should be. Authenticity requires vulnerability; you must be willing to act according to your true nature, even when you feel uncomfortable. Embrace aspects of yourself you tend to suppress or hide, along with those you love.

Authenticity starts when you set the intention to be genuine. Set an intention to always speak your truth. This was, and is still, one of my biggest hurdles. It's often difficult to speak your truth, but when you do, it will be incredibly liberating.

There's no shortcut to finding out who you really are. Being authentic can be a life-long journey.

2. Find Your Passion

Think back to the question you were asked by every long-lost relative at every family function until the age of eighteen: What do you want to be when you grow up? Create some space to rediscover what puts fire in your belly, what makes your heart race. Often we know what we don't want, but now ask yourself what you really do want.

After discovering transformational author Janet Bray Attwood's Passion Test, I rediscovered my passion for writing—not writing about daily crimes and politics, but life and how other people navigate their way through it. I'd buried away my love of this for years because of financial and family commitments.

Now is the time to uncover your passion. Unleash it. Follow it. Don't let fear hold you back. Take some quiet time to think what you absolutely love doing. Don't worry about what others will think; it's time to be true to yourself. Once you find your passion and start practicing it, you'll begin to put some joy back into your life.

3. Be Grateful

The simple act of being grateful can provide a truckload of benefits. Countless scientific studies have shown that being grateful on a daily basis can make you feel more optimistic about all areas of your life.

It's been my daily practice to write in my gratitude journal every day, without missing a beat. At first, I viewed it as my own social experiment, but after witnessing the change in my life, I have felt its amazing impact.

The benefits of this daily practice have been slow but powerful. I am more hopeful about my future, calmer, and more loving. I'm exercising regularly and enjoying stronger, more meaningful friendships.

Practice being grateful by keeping a notebook beside your bed and each night writing down four or five aspects of your day or life you can be thankful for. Challenge yourself by not repeating items from previous days so you will find smaller things for which to be grateful, such as a smile from a stranger, or feeling the sand underneath your toes.

4. Tell the Universe What You *Really* Want

I'd always believed setting goals was not for me. They seemed too difficult to achieve. I'd read countless articles on how goal setting worked for high achievers, so why couldn't I get it to work for me? I'd tried over and over, and every time I failed.

My goals always seemed to be the earth-shattering, life-changing type, with ridiculous deadlines.

So now I set intentions rather than goals. The magic in setting intentions is to be specific. For example, don't just say, "I want an abundant life." Clarify which parts of your life you want to be abundant. Is it more money, better relationships, or job satisfaction? Look to the future, not the past, and focus on what your life will look and feel like when you achieve your intention.

Be determined! Those who keep pressing ahead will be successful.

5. Write a Bucket List

Do you have a list all the things you'd love to accomplish before it's too late?

Compiling a bucket list is a simple way to help you focus. It can also be a springboard to achieving what you really want in life and discovering what you really value. Ticking items off your list and getting friends and family to share them with you will bring fun and joy into your life.

6. Create a Vision Board

After interviewing successful people, I've discovered that one common trait they share is visualizing their fame, fortune, or achievements. From building multimillion-dollar businesses to losing weight or winning an Olympic gold medal, they use a number of visual techniques to make it happen.

The mental practice of visualization can get you closer to where you want to be in life and prepare you for success. Research shows that adding a visual component to goal setting can significantly change the outcome.

Creating a vision board is one way to envision your success or life's desires. My vision board is full of pictures and words of how my wonderful life is going to look. It's taped to the wardrobe doors so I see it immediately when I wake up and just before I go to bed.

To create my vision board I sit quietly in front of my computer and imagine what I want in my life, now and in the future. I visualize feelings, words, or material possessions and find images that represent that vision.

When making a vision board, use your intuition to help you find pictures and words. Don't think too much about which ones you like but pay attention to how they make you feel.

As you receive or manifest your desires on the vision board, always be thankful for them. As mentioned above, practicing gratitude will bring more good things.

Anita Catalano has been a journalist at some of Australia's most prestigious newspapers.

Instead of writing about other people's lives, a few years ago Anita knew it was time to turn the spotlight on herself and share her journey as she muddled her way through the breakup of her marriage, motherhood, and maturity.

From meditating with shamans in the Arizona desert to riding her Vespa along the coast of Australia, Anita's stylish pilgrimage is still a work in progress. She'll teach you how to find that pot of spiritual gold…and do it in your favorite dress and high heels!

If you love the idea of a cheeky read and relate to a forty-something woman/ex-wife/mom who embarks on a sometimes amusing journey to "find herself," you'll love Anita's book, A Pilgrim in Prada. *It's an* Eat Pray Love *for Baby Boomers!*

Connect with Anita at www.anitacatalano.com.

Chapter 13

Lost and Found

EM Richter

I have a confession to make.

I've been hiding this secret for a long time.

I'm finally ready to reveal that the secret is this: I get lost.

Directionally, deliberately, deliciously lost. No matter where I wander in the world I find myself wondering where I am.

Don't get me wrong. It's not that I don't know how to follow directions or that I'm purposely sabotaging myself. Or, perhaps I am. Perhaps I enjoy the time of not knowing most of all.

For me, a destination is not a finish line to cross, but rather, a desire, a feeling of connection to an ultimate goal. A destination serves me as a blueprint, not the indelible mark of a fingerprint.

Even as a child, I would delightedly wander in a dream-like state, much to my mother's dismay. I remember once wading into the shallow waters of the sea, my mother blissfully reclined in a beach chair, toes curled into the water-kissed sand, as the tug of the waves carried my little body farther and farther away from the shore. My mother's panicked yells awoke me from my momentary reverie, but I wasn't bothered because I was magically carried away in my own dream world.

As I grew up and began to travel the world, my sense of adventure and wanderlust overrode my need for direction. I got off course in the Munich train system and discovered an impromptu jazz concert in a majestic garden. Getting lost in Mexico for a week found me in an unexpected Cinco de Mayo celebration. Getting on the wrong bus on route to the Taj Mahal led to me being sari-clad in a local wedding ceremony.

My day-to-day directional challenges allow me to make friends and close connections around the world. Holding my destination loosely opens up a world of synchronicity; getting lost in my daydreams lets my imagination jump from one dimension to another.

As a kid, I remember feeling disconnected from the world outside of me. The only real connection I had was with the fantasies I created in my head, to the books I read or the characters I conceived. I remember feeling crestfallen frustration with the people around me, mired in their constrictive realities because I preferred the infiniteness of my daydreams. I created my world, and in that world I wasn't a shy and awkward girl with a lisp. In my world I was extroverted, confident, and popular. In my world, the rules of social conduct didn't apply to me. In my world, I made up the rules as I went along. And as I grew, I came to realize that my fantasy created my reality. By not following the social rules, I allowed myself to follow the messages of my intuition.

True direction means existing without the rulebook and the limitations it creates.

Sometimes, when I find myself following the rules instead of my inner urges, I remind myself to check in with my "little girl delightfully lost." If I find that there is a lack of integrity in my life, then I know that I have wandered into Got-To-Get-There Territory rather than toward

Wonder Town. There's always that telltale discomfort that's impossible to ignore, the punch in the gut I get when I'm doing something for any other reason than creative energy. The outpouring of energy leaves me feeling like a bird in a cage, trapped and tethered.

Ignoring our inner guidance system, in essence, is a denial of who we are. Striving to reach a preplanned destination, a finish line, a preset route, takes us way off course from creating our own limitless realities.

Some people like to goal set.

I prefer to soul get.

There are a few simple things you can do to break all the rules and build a life full of wonder.

Make Up Stories, but Know Your Truth

Don't lie to yourself just so you can continue to live against your own internal desires. If you hate your job, ask yourself why you're really there. If you aren't in ecstatic love with your partner, get real about why you're still in the relationship. If you dislike any part of your body, acknowledge the dislike for that body part without judging your whole being. Take stock of the unwanted circumstances in your life and ask yourself why you keep choosing them. While you're telling yourself the story of your life start with the words "I choose…"

Tell Powerful Stories

Shifting your story is as easy as 1, 2, 3. Try this three-step formula to shift your story from merely positive thinking to powerful feeling.

1. **Notice it.** Have the courage to be honest with yourself about what you're truly feeling in you're experience.
2. **Name it.** Name the story you would like to retell just as you would name a project or theme. You could have a Year without Fear if you want to add some courage to your life. Or, if you

want to reconnect with an aspect of you that feels lost, why not name it Finding Me-Now? Maybe Good Thrill Hunting will be the mantra you choose for some adventure and exploration.

3. **Neutralize it.** Now put your story into a new and exciting context. Visualize your new story as words printed on a T-shirt (kind of like the scene from *Forrest Gump*), or a caption on a birthday card, a slogan on a billboard, graffiti on a wall. You could say the words in a foreign accent, or sing the words to the tune of a song ("Twinkle, Twinkle, Little Star" works well). You can picture the thoughts as a scroll or as movie credits, or as stickers on a suitcase, or as bumper stickers on cars driving by. Whatever the mode you choose to retell your new story, just remember to make it fun.

Decide to Feel Good

Begin to fantasize about scenarios that make you purr like a kitten. Daydream about your dream job. What would you do? Who would you meet? What would you wear? Romanticize the perfect romance. Where would the two of you go together? How would it feel to swoon in adoration? What would you say to your beloved? Become entranced with your physical body. What heightened senses does it respond to? What energy does your body radiate? What magnetism does your body emit?

Put Your Intuition into Fruition!

Create your new story into the world of reality. This is an ancient technique passed down by the great sages of the past. When you follow all the rules, you often fail to see situations as gifts and opportunities for growth. Telling yourself the story of your bad times and perceiving it as a negative situation, you block the flow of magnetic energy. You make it impossible for new realities to unfold because of the minefield of mental debris. Clear up the psychic cloud by using your imagination and cutting the cords that have been caging you. When you rewrite the story of your personal history into an ideal fantasy, you create an environment in which to see the situation as your greatest growth.

Stop Dreaming and Start Doing!

I spent so much time fantasizing when I was young, but until I embraced those dreams into the fold of my reality, they remained elusive. Because when I was only in "thinking mode," I didn't get to the doing and the creating; therefore, I missed the essential ingredient that grows confidence. I missed putting deed before creed. Until I combined my actions with my dreams I was following a perpetual loop of separating my life from all of those rules that I disdained. Marrying your dreams to your reality breeds your confidence.

Whatever you can think to do to make your dreams real, begin it now. And allow yourself to get wonderfully, wondrously, willfully lost.

Because not all who wander are lost.

EM Richter is the author of The Secret of the Storyteller: A Novel of Awakening *and* Brave Ecstatic Woman: Igniting Your Feminine Essence for an Audaciously Luscious Life.

To find out which one of the Seven Feminine Archetypes you are and to download free Brave Ecstatic Woman: The Playbook *straight to your inbox go to www.braveecstaticwoman.com or visit EM at www.emrichter.com for weekly tips and techniques, not-so-random musings, and other fun goodies.*

Chapter 14

Born Confident

Katharine Bain

I've noticed that some people seem to have limitless self-confidence. Situations that you or I might find intimidating, if not downright terrifying, these people face without blinking an eye.

"Will you give this speech?" they're asked. Sure!

Take on new duties at work? You bet!

Ask that beautiful girl (or knock-'em-dead handsome guy) out on a date? Of course!

Where do these people get all this confidence? Is there a website where they just order it up every week? Or what?

Well, maybe it's not such a mystery. After all, there is one segment of the population where limitless confidence is the norm, not the exception: young children.

Given how important confidence is to help us to get what we want and need, it's worthwhile to take a close look at these little confidence machines.

Learning from Birth to Age Five

A different perspective is probably helpful in this important area of our lives, so let's examine a powerful reality about confidence readily available for us to study.

We know that a newborn baby registers the environment with all his (or her) senses, yet the baby's brain is not registering stimuli in the ways that an adult brain would. The baby has not yet learned what these sensory impulses mean. Isn't it interesting to note that a newborn baby has eyes, ears, a nose, a tongue, and fingers and toes and does not experience seeing, hearing, smelling, tasting, and touching the way he will later learn to do?

It takes this innocent and quite marvelous child quite a long time to learn to see. In the meantime, the child's parents put their faces right in front of the baby's face and smile and talk to get their baby's attention. Eventually they're rewarded when their little baby smiles back at Mommy and Daddy. What a happy memory!

How long does this learning to smile process take? It can take six to eight weeks. Wow! How can such a simple thing take so long? It's especially fascinating when we consider that a foal (baby horse) learns to stand on its long, wobbly legs within an hour of birth so that it can begin to nurse from its mother.

And yet, look at how much this tiny infant is learning all at once. So many stimuli are all streaming into the baby's brain. This precious child has to learn so many things—seeing, hearing, tasting, smelling, feeling, lifting up his head, rolling over, sitting up, what water is when you give him a bath, what the sound is when your dog barks, crawling, walking, jumping, running, turning, twirling, and let's not forget talking. Where is your nose? Where is your ear? What color is this? Where's sister Lisa? Any baby's to-do list is enormous!

Confidence to Learn

The question is not how you, like everyone else, learned all of this more quickly than you'll ever learn during the rest of your life. The question is how did you have the confidence to learn so much so fast?!?

Do you remember lying in your crib and fretting about whether you were ever going to be able to learn how to turn over? Did you worry endlessly about finding where your nose was? Were you wondering if all the other babies were going to be able to crawl before you did? Did you have worry lines on your forehead about learning colors and being afraid you would never pass the color test? My gosh, it's all enough to ensure that you would never want to leave your crib! Did the world not realize the pressure you were under to know all this before you were even five years old?!?

Of course the world didn't realize this. The fact is that you were not the least bit intimidated by the notion of learning. You just did what you felt like and most of what you learned came under the category of play. Patty Cake, Patty Cake was fun when you learned it. And all the other learning experiences were too.

Born to Be Confident

The learning in your first five years was effortless. Why should it be different now? The innate tendency to acquire confidence is built into small children as they explore their world and expand their territory. Validation from caregivers encourages them.

Lest you doubt this reality, I invite you to observe a group of four- or five-year-old children. If they are left alone, their play might develop into confrontation based on conflicting needs. However, in a situation with a teacher guiding their activities, we can see a very positive atmosphere. See them all talking to each other. Notice how unafraid they are to offer their ideas to the other children. See them talking and laughing with no judgement or criticism. (And remember Art Linkletter's *Kids Say the Darndest Things*.)

A Real Example of a Young Child's Confidence

I remember experiencing firsthand the indomitable confidence of a four-year-old and being amazed by it. My father was one of twelve children, nine of them boys, and they all lived in a big L-shaped house out in the country. There was a huge lawn around the Big House. Between the house and the old chicken coop, out the back door, through the garden, and quite a distance from the Big House was the swimming pool. For a private pool, it was quite large, twenty yards long and ten yards wide with a diving board at the deep end.

I particularly recall this one beautiful summer day watching numerous cousins of all ages and sizes cavorting happily in the cool water of this beautiful blue pool. Brown-as-a-berry Jason, four years old; our slim, 6' 7" cousin Scott, eighteen; and I, age sixteen, were all standing at the end of the pool when Scott and I became aware that Jason was not happy.

"Scott, I sure wish I knew how to swim. It looks like so much fun." Jason knew that Scott was a competitive swimmer and idolized him for many reasons. Scott heard the disappointment in his voice and encouraged Jason to jump in the pool by demonstrating the arm and leg movements Jason could use to swim. Jason looked dubious about these instructions and voiced a very valid concern, "But, Scott, what if I drown?"

At this Scott grinned down at Jason and replied, "Jason, do you think I would just stand here and let you drown?"

Thinking about it for a moment, Jason apparently convinced himself of the truth of Scott's statement, so he walked confidently to the edge of the pool, bent his knees and threw himself as far as he could into the water. I was astounded to see this four-year-old nonswimmer demonstrate such faith and, yes, frightening confidence. Sinking far beneath the surface did not faze Jason. He followed Scott's brief instructions and seemed intuitively to know when to breathe as he bobbed his way up and down until he reached the side of the pool.

Scott and I stepped up to the pool's edge as we watched Jason's slow but steady progress. We both knelt down as he got closer. When Jason reached the side of the pool, he wiped the water out of his eyes so he could see and looked up. Scott was right there with a big grin on his face. "See, Jason, you can swim." What a complex skill to learn in mere seconds! What an accomplishment! Jason was pumped. And I was truly delighted to have witnessed such a wonderful example of the confidence that faith and trust confer on us.

Jason's trust in Scott, buttressed by Scott's faith in Jason's ability, propelled him into that pool at the age of four even though he had never swum before in his life. We are born with all the confidence we need. It's all around us. I invite you to check it out for yourself.

Not "How Can I Get It" but "Where Did It Go"?

Still, when most of us look at the issue of confidence and feel that we need more of it to accomplish the very important goals in our lives, we usually ask a number of questions. *How can I become more confident? Who can help me? Will it take a lot of time and money? What will people think?*

But the critical question is, *What happened to the innate ability to try anything with which I was born?* As a child you never worried about whether you could learn all the things that most children do learn. You already knew "Just do it!" Neither risk nor lack of confidence was a big factor in your decision-making process. Without opposition, most of us act out of our inborn confidence.

Charlie Brown Adults

Do you remember the Charlie Brown programs we all watched on TV as kids? What were those adults always saying? "Squawk! Squawk! Squawk!" When we are very young, we live in our own worlds, don't we? Parents exist but only to satisfy our needs. We don't hear them.

It's not until we get older and our needs and the needs of our parents start to diverge that the problem begins. What problem? The myriad conflicts that eventually lead to loss of confidence.

We Wonder What Is Wrong with Us
as We Experience Daily Criticism

As you grow, your parents begin to expect more from you. They start to expect you to honor boundaries. These boundaries restrict your behavior. In your constant desire to have fun, you didn't like those boundaries. And why should you? It is totally normal to want to have fun, to want to do whatever comes into your mind to see if you like it.

As children, we follow our passions. It's the obvious and reasonable course to follow. Actually, if you think about it as an adult, wouldn't you like to have fun all the time too? Of course you would.

However, as an adult you can now understand why your parents got frustrated when they found you had finger painted all over the beautiful living room wallpaper. You can relate to their desire then for you to play *quietly* inside for one bitterly cold, boring winter day after another.

As children what do you remember hearing? Maybe things like "Don't do that." "I told you not to..." "Why don't you stop when I tell you to?" "How many times do I have to tell you...?"

Emotional Overtones

Not only do you hear the words over and over again, but you also hear the tones. Even though you were only a child, still on a deep level you knew very well that your very survival depended on your parents.

When we are children we are very defenseless and emotionally vulnerable. We have no protection. The tones of voice and the expressions of annoyance, frustration, impatience, and, even more, outright anger are a tsunami of anxiety for a small child. As children we begin, and continue, to receive the message that we are not just doing something wrong. We begin to believe that we are wrong. Ouch!

Further, you experience those negative emotional overtones surrounding the words of complaint as separation from the people most important to you. That is intensely painful too. The weight of these negative emotions dumped on you reduces your energy level and makes you feel bad about yourself.

As an adult you can look back and easily see that there was nothing wrong with you. You were just being who you are and doing what came naturally. Wouldn't you do the same thing now if you could?

We are prevented from doing so today by two major restrictions. One is responsibilities, which show up in so many ways. Among them are responsibilities to family, to career, to societal norms, to religious beliefs. The other restriction is the one caused by having, as a child, your innate exuberance toward life stifled. That exuberance and the desire to be and do caused the criticism that eventually may have made you feel bad about yourself. Did your parents do this on purpose? Of course not. Did they even know they were doing this? No. Still, did it happen to most of us? Yes. Did that affect our confidence? Likely it did.

Of course it is an entirely different story when caregivers are actually abusive. Then the messages are much more strongly worded and may even include violence. It is easy to understand why a child in those circumstances may wash up on the shores of his teenage years sullen and resentful.

And yet the constant negative programming of children with parents who are the most loving and well meaning in the world can still make those children feel less than they were when they were very young.

What Can You Do?

If these concepts feel true, then isn't it time to ask yourself, *What happened to my confidence?* I suggest that it is just where you left it. It's not a matter of developing it or creating it, at a cost of much time and money. It's a matter of uncovering it.

The desire to have fun still resides within us. That desire is already a strong and powerful force in your life. I suggest that it is time to explore any attitudes that may have obscured that desire and the confidence that accompanies it. It is there waiting for you. As Dale Carnegie said, "Change your mind. Change your life." You were born with the desire to have fun, to feel passion. You were *born confident!* Uncover that confidence. Move forward in your life.

Oh, by the way, did Jason have the fun he thought he would as a swimmer? He certainly did. He had a blast!

 *Katharine Bain*, BSc (math), founded a thirty-year financial institution in Canada. *Life crises powerfully led to service as a financial advisor. Numerous clients taught her that true abundance is a mind-set before a bank account. Katharine was a director of her national professional association for its first five years, has been widely quoted nationally, and* moderated a five-year TV program.

Katharine's PhD in life experience is her most valuable degree. She believes we all have a mission. Hers is to guide very wealthy men from surprising, perplexing despair to a life of exciting promise. Please visit www. modernmidas.solutions.

Chapter 15

Discover the Art of
Freedom—and Thrive!

Everything can be taken from a man but one thing: the last of the human freedoms—to choose one's attitude in any given set of circumstances, to choose one's own way.
—Viktor E. Frankl

H ow did I get here?" Flat on my back, paralyzed with anxiety, I was looking up at the world from the floor. Everything had turned completely upside down. It was early in '08 and my life had crashed from "I got this" to "What the hell happened?"

Just six months before this day, I had believed that everything was under control. My wife, Sarah, and I were happily married, and I owned a successful real estate development company with five amazing employees. We were developing three great projects, which, all told, had a projected value of over $20 million. Two of them were doing great; the other, a residential housing development, was moving more slowly than I had anticipated due to red tape bogging down the process and increasing the budget. But all was good.

"I got this" was my mantra. Every day, when new challenges arose, I said this to myself and kept moving forward. There was no problem too big for me to handle.

Then, in July of '07, my wife Sarah found a lump in her breast. One day she was sitting at our dining table, and when she reached up to scratch an itch, she felt something that didn't belong there. What followed was a blur of doctors' appointments and consultations, examinations and procedures, ending finally in our sitting in the doctor's office awaiting the results of a biopsy. The doctor came into the office and wouldn't look Sarah in the eye. He was nervous. And then came the word that you never want to hear: "cancer." That word holds such power. It's the only clear memory I have of that day. My wife has cancer…

"We got this," I told her. "I am here to support you in any way I can." For the next two years I was by her side for surgery, chemotherapy, and finally radiation. I couldn't imagine being anywhere else. She was incredibly brave and strong, and I wanted to be at every appointment to support her as she battled this dreaded disease.

While this was going on, a steady drumbeat of bad news was sounding daily. The economy was failing, and it was failing fast. The housing bubble was collapsing, and it showed every indication of taking everything down with it. As I sat by Sarah's side, I watched the news and a terrible foreboding arose in me. I tried to fight it off.

"I got this," I told myself. "We'll get these houses done and on the market before things turn really bad." But as the days went by, it became all too clear that there was no way to make that happen. My biggest project was going to go down in flames along with the economy, and there was nothing I could do to stop it. I saw the future and it wasn't pretty. Everything we had was invested in these projects.

At the time our sons were eight and twelve. My biggest worry was protecting them from the fear and anxiety that was beginning to occupy me most of the time. I did everything I could to keep them assured. "Mom's going to be fine, guys," I told them. I tried to hide the stress I felt every day as I went to the office and fought an impossible battle to keep the company afloat.

My typical day consisted of caring for our sons, shuttling Sarah to chemo and doctors' appointments, and then trudging to the office for meetings and phone calls with lawyers and bankers who were getting more and more aggressive as the financial news got worse and worse. My life felt like a living nightmare.

"I got this," I repeated over and over and over, willing it to be true.

Then one day the load of stress, fear, and anxiety overwhelmed me. I was in our bedroom, about to head out to pick up our sons from school when, out of the blue, I collapsed. Without warning, my legs gave way and I fell to the floor as if paralyzed. I don't know how long I was down there before I became aware of what had happened. I just remember looking up and asking myself, "How did I get here?"

Well, sometimes it takes a complete change in your perspective to see things in a new way. As I lay there on the bedroom carpet, I began a dialogue with myself: "How did you get here?" turned into "Now what?" and then, "Michael, your sons need you. How are you going to take care of them from down here?"

In that moment, in a flash of insight, I realized something so simple and yet so profound: It was not the actual problems that were weighing me down. It was the fears, doubts, worries, and anxieties *about* the problems that had led to my exhaustion and collapse. The problems were big, for sure. But each one, taken on its own, could be addressed. It was the ceaseless refrain of what ifs, worries, and worst-case scenarios in my head that was killing me.

And suddenly I saw my mistake so clearly. I had been seeing only problems to be solved, so everywhere I looked there were only problems. Big problems. And I took on each and every one with my vow that "I got this," until I felt like Atlas carrying the world on my shoulders. But as a mere mortal I could not bear that weight.

My mistake was that I had lost sight of the path, and I had surrendered my power to choose how I wanted to respond to these incredible challenges. My whole life I had been a problem solver, and I had become an expert at finding problems to solve. But what if there was another way?

Wow, I thought. *Could I possibly* choose *my response to what life hands me—no matter what circumstances were bearing down on me?*

Could I do my best to create the circumstances I wanted and, at the same time, accept that I couldn't choose what happened in my life, just my response to it?

Was this even possible? I didn't know at the time, but I was determined to find out.

Thus began five years of research and learning, diving deep into the study of prosperity, metaphysics, spirituality, and personal development. I traveled thousands of miles and spent countless hours soaking up these teachings like a sponge. And I'm happy to report that, *yes,* it is possible to choose your response to bad or even terrifying events. And even more importantly, it is possible to create a life of total freedom, liberated from the sabotaging effects of fear, doubt, worry, and anxiety.

Today, I am happy to report, my two sons are thriving and Sarah is healthier than ever. None of the most dreaded outcomes ever came to be. I have taken my entrepreneurial skills and transferred them from developing buildings to creating a company that helps people build their lives. And, despite my fear that everything would be lost, I ended up discovering one of the greatest secrets of the universe: *You are free to create your life and choose your state of consciousness, no matter what circumstances you find yourself in.*

Living this truth is living the Art of Freedom. *You* determine your reality, based on the thoughts and beliefs that you hold in your mind and what you choose to put your attention on. Ultimately, you have two choices: You can focus on the path, or you can focus on the obstacle. And whatever you focus on grows. If your attention is on the obstacle, you will be blocked and unable to progress. If, however, you see only the path, you will inevitably be able to navigate toward your dreams and arrive at your destination.

As I've lived with and integrated this awareness, I've discovered the keys to limitless creativity and manifestation and created a life of complete freedom for myself. And perhaps the greatest gift has been the ability to teach others how to do the same. With the perspective of time, I've been able to identify four key actions for you to follow. I'm happy to say that if you follow these simple suggestions, you too can live a life of freedom and thrive, no matter what life is throwing at you.

The Four Keys to Freedom

Key 1: Focus on the good in your life and give thanks

Yep, that's right. No matter what challenges you're facing right now, there is something or someone near you to be grateful for. And what we focus on grows. In my dark days I was focusing on the problems and the fears, and, as a result I was surrounded by problems and fears. After my wake-up call, I realized that despite the huge challenges I faced, I had a lot to be thankful for. First and foremost was the love I had for Sarah and our two sons. There were many days when the only thing that kept me moving forward was that love. And the more I was grateful for the joy they brought to my life, the easier it became to find joy in other areas of my life as well.

Daily practice: Start a daily habit of finding gratitude for what you have in your life right now. Always be on the lookout for new things, relevant to the day's challenges and gifts, to keep it fresh. You could join the hundreds of people who have done the Twenty-one-Day Gratitude Challenge. This is my gift to you. (See the link at the end of this chapter for more information.)

Key 2: Keep your attention on what you want more of in your life

This is related to the first step. Too often we're focused on what we *don't* want that's appearing in our lives. That can leave us surrounded by fear and doubt and the dreaded prospect of failure. And like a moth attracted to the flame, if we stare at it, we are drawn right to what we do not want.

We have to keep what we *do* want foremost in our awareness. When I get ready to take a trip, I know exactly where I want to go. If I want to visit my mother in LA, I have to plan out every step of a trip that ultimately gets me to Los Angeles. Manifestation works in much the same way. I can't create something that I can't visualize. Or, as one of my metaphysics teachers taught me: "What happens in vagueness stays in vagueness." And vagueness doesn't manifest results!

Daily practice: Keep your eye on the goal. Spend fifteen minutes in meditation visualizing your ideal life every day. Enjoy imagining every detail, and afterward record in a journal what you saw. Write it out in the present tense as if it already exists.

Key 3: Don't let the obstacles distract you

As you proceed along the path toward your dreams and visions, obstacles will arise—that's a given. And it's very important that you see the obstacles and address the crucial ones, but you do not want to dwell on them. It's all too easy to focus on them and lose sight of your destination, in which case progress stops and inertia kicks in.

You want to keep your eye on the path, not on the obstacles along the way, because we tend to steer toward what we focus on. If you're driving down the road and an obstacle appears ahead of you and it's all you can see, you likely will end up steering directly toward it and hitting it. So, as soon as you see an obstacle to your goals, identify it, deal with it, and then shift your attention to the path around it. In doing so, you'll keep your eye on the solution, not the problem.

Daily practice: Write out a plan for achieving your vision and revisit it daily. Focus on what action needs to be taken today. Take on your problems one by one and be sure to make progress toward your dream every day.

Key 4: Release and replace old beliefs

Old beliefs and behaviors do pop up, and they can sabotage your success. Many are subconscious and trigger unconscious responses to stressful situations. They can be subtle and difficult to identify, but they're there and, if left unchecked, will continue to block your progress.

So, how do you identify these subconscious beliefs, which, by definition, are beyond our conscious awareness? Here's the trick: We can't always identify the belief, but we can know it by its undesired results. Ever notice that the same unwanted outcome keeps appearing over and over again in your life? That outcome is being created by a sabotaging belief buried deep in the subconscious.

These beliefs, often implanted long ago by parents, teachers, or the media, tell us that we are not worthy, capable, or creative, or countless other limiting ideas that blind us to our unlimited divine power. But the truth is just the opposite! You *are* worthy, capable, creative, and immensely powerful—more powerful than you can imagine until you shift your awareness and, ultimately, your beliefs.

Daily practice: In your journal, write down one or more undesired outcomes in your life right now. Then write a response to this question:

What belief is causing this to occur right now? Write down the false beliefs that arise. A false belief is anything that doesn't empower you or that doesn't validate your divine nature. Then write down a new, supportive belief that will empower you to create your vision. Post this belief where you can see it frequently throughout the day. Make it your new mantra.

• • •

These four keys will free you from your old sabotaging beliefs, I guarantee it—*but only if you use them!* And by use them, I mean seriously commit to practicing them every single day. Along with meditation, prayer, exercise, and healthy eating, they will produce great changes in your life, but only if you apply them in an intentional and consistent way. Write them into your daily schedule and make them your very top priority! They are the basic building blocks of your success.

Over time the practice will become a natural and enjoyable part of your routine, and you'll notice that the old, debilitating beliefs are falling away. And what replaces them? The powerful knowingness that what you desire is right here, just waiting for you to claim it. Take action based on *that* liberating belief, and you—and everything in your life—will thrive!

A creator at heart, Michael LeValley started working in theater at the age of sixteen. Later he started his own design studio and built handcrafted furniture. His next (and most rewarding) creative project was raising his two sons as a stay-at-home dad.

Michael went on to develop two artist studio complexes in northern California. He has also coached creative professionals and business owners in realizing their dreams.

In 2014 Michael launched the Art of Freedom community. Michael is passionate about inspiring and instructing others to live lives of complete freedom. For more information about the Art of Freedom, join us on Facebook at www.facebook.com/theartoffreedomcommunity and visit www. theartoffreedom.com.

Chapter 16

Mother Mary's Tips for
Parenting from Love, Not Fear

Tracey Souverein

There we were, sitting behind the fence, happily watching our boys congratulate each other after another baseball win—and the next minute, they were besieging us, asking for an energy drink or caffeine burst to make it through the next game. Since when did kids stop being tireless Energizer Bunnies from dawn to dusk?

Well, probably since we started expecting them to play more games in one day than professionals. These boys were heading into their third game, and if they won it, there would be another—all in one day! I was exhausted just sitting and watching them, so I could totally imagine their own exhaustion. It got me thinking: maybe these kids' batteries began to run low long ago.

Today's kids have been overloaded with lessons, from foreign-language videos for babies, to toddler violin classes, to sports training camps for preteens. Sadly, more and more often I hear parents tell their kids, "Sorry, there just isn't any time for a play date today!" Isn't unstructured time to play with friends what childhood is all about? What's the purpose of all this activity? Must there be relentless pressure for parents to produce extraordinary kids, and for kids to meet their expectations?

Now, believe me, I understand. Who among us doesn't want the absolute very best lives for our children? Parents dream of their kids using their knowledge, strength, and kind hearts to help make the world a better place—perhaps even a bit more like heaven. But in our efforts to help them use their God-given gifts fully, have we lost our trust in those gifts—and the Giver?

Look at the results of our efforts to create extraordinary kids:

- Bullying has become commonplace as kids attempt to feel better than others. According to a UCLA study, 83 percent of girls and 79 percent of boys in middle school reported having being bullied, either in person or online.

- Researchers at Columbia University say preteens and teens from affluent, well-educated families have the highest rates of depression, substance abuse, anxiety disorders, and unhappiness of any group of children in the United States.

- Kids are injuring themselves more seriously than ever. Forty percent of all sports-related injuries treated in hospitals are to children from the ages of five to fourteen.

- And, most concerning of all, some kids lack the knowledge and the confidence to act without a parent, teacher, or coach telling them what to do. One study, by educational psychologist Kyung-Hee Kim, showed children have become "less energetic, less talkative and verbally expressive, less imaginative, and less perceptive," making it difficult for them to play creatively on their own.

This generation of children is so over-coached into becoming super-charged kids that they have become fearful of failing and of expressing their true selves. And all so they can perform to levels well beyond what was expected of our generation. What does that matter if they aren't happy?

I believe the key mistake we've been making is this: We've been measuring our children from what can be seen on the outside—basically, their performance in school, sports, and life—when our primary focus should be on appreciating and nurturing the goodness we see within them.

A wonderful example of a parent doing this was given by the mother of one of the most amazing men to ever live, one who changed humanity forever with his faith, hope, and love. I turned to Mother Mary, the mother of Jesus, to learn how to parent extraordinary children.

I began looking to Mother Mary as an example when my firstborn was what they called "colicky" back then. He cried nonstop, sleeping only for short bits throughout the day and night, and he needed to be held constantly. Colic, they said, usually lasts three months—my son's lasted for years. As I was searching for a way to soothe him, I was constantly asking God, "How do I parent this precious little boy?" I tried to relate to God as a parent because He knows all and I felt like I knew nothing!

These were the days when "What would Jesus do?" was becoming a common phrase, but that didn't work for me in this case because Jesus wasn't a parent, let alone a mother! What I did learn about parenting from Jesus's words was that whatever we do to the least of our brothers and sisters, we have done to him. I realized that I would serve my children best by treating them as I would treat Jesus if he were my child—and that's when I began to think of his mother, Mary.

Mary was a human and a mother, so she had surely endured sleepless nights with an infant, consoled a crying toddler, struggled to discipline an active child and direct a teenager, and finally come to terms with her son's choices and role in God's plan as an adult. She was someone I could relate to, and my journey as a parent became easier, and more successful, when I began to follow her lead.

In some ways, I see parallels between her way of parenting and our current way. Did Mother Mary send Jesus to rigorous training for his body, mind, and spirit to become a model for love and forgiveness? Actually, she did! Ancient texts from India and other lands provide evidence that Jesus spent time from ages twelve to thirty learning from the spiritual masters, saints, and wise men of the Far East. So we are aligned with Mary's actions when we seek quality education and training for our children.

And, did Jesus also experience great pressure to perform to his full potential? Oh, not too much—only that everywhere he went people were expecting miracles from him! And this is despite Jesus's proclamation that it was the people who healed themselves through their own faith. Nonetheless, he was held responsible for many things that were out of his control. Talk about pressure!

Also, his very first public miracle came at his mother's encouragement. Mother Mary's suggestion that Jesus seize the opportunity to reveal his true nature led to his first miracle at the wedding in Cana. And, just like our own kids, Jesus argued that he was not ready to do so!

So, Jesus did face many of the same pressures of today's children, and of course, far more. But look at the primary difference between Mother Mary's parenting and ours today: She had unwavering faith in the spirit of God within her son. She allowed that spirit, that power of God within Jesus, to be illuminated in all that Jesus did.

Easy for her, you say. God told her that her son was His child! But Jesus's message was that we are all God's children. We all equally have the spirit of God within us, just as he did. So, bear with me, and try to keep a straight face as I give you the following suggestion: Just imagine if your child were Jesus Christ—minus the robe and halo. Just wearing his soccer uniform or her pink tutu. Knowing that the spirit of God was within her, would you be so quick to direct her interests? Would you be so quick to judge his abilities and worry whether he was on the right path? What would you attempt to teach her? How would you spend time with him? How would you respond to his cries, his anger, his joy? Who would you surround her with? Where would you take her?

These are the questions that reeled through my mind when I first became a mother myself and sought parenting help from the divine.

I spent the next fifteen years researching Mary's life, looking for insight into her ways of parenting as I raised my sons. It wasn't easy because, as important as she is, she is rarely mentioned in the Bible. In my search, I found mystical accounts of her life, theological studies, Gnostic gospels, knowledge of the Essene ways of living, reports of apparitions, and more. Between my research and my prayers, my parenting motto became "What would Mother Mary do?"

She did brilliant things. Most significantly, Mother Mary nurtured what I call "the Light Within" her child. It is my belief that there is a light of God's goodness, perfection, and pure knowledge within each of us, and, as parents, we are called to nurture that light to shine brightly. This, I believe, is the core of her approach to raising Jesus. As he tells us, "The kingdom of God is within you" (Luke 17:21, KJV). Mother Mary believed that and also that the light of that kingdom of God can be nurtured through unconditional love.

Here are some of the main lessons I've learned from Mother Mary about how to nurture the Light Within our children.

Come from Love, Not from Fear

There is no fear in love; but perfect love casts out fear, because fear involves punishment and the one who fears is not perfected in love.
—**1 John 4:18** (NASB)

Mother Mary wanted Jesus to be motivated by love. Love feels good and brings joy; love is patient and kind and removes all fear. Parents are filled with fear these days as our immersion in media has kept us all hyperaware of every threat to our kids' well-being. The world seems more dangerous and competitive than ever, and as a result, our kids are motivated more from a place of fear than from a place of love.

But parenting from fear leads us into a world of judgment that separates us from God. God is love, which is acceptance and appreciation—the very opposite of judgment. Today's kids constantly feel judged, and fear that if they don't live up to expectations, they will be denied love, acceptance, good grades, playing time, advancement to the next level of courses…and the list goes on. And that feeling of being judged puts a cover over the Light Within.

Every time you make the choice to parent from love, fear is removed because trust grows. As you move in the direction of perfect love, you develop an overwhelming sense of trust that God is with you and on your side. Knowing that He desires for you every good thing you desire for yourself, you can be free of fear and able to love.

Encouragement, Instead of Praise

According to Jewish law, one must never say anything about a person or judge a person in any way. Even to say something good about someone in front of another can lead to jealousy and, therefore, potential harm. So Mother Mary must have offered encouragement rather than praise when raising Jesus, as many recommend today.

Encouragement focuses on the child's internal feelings and motivation, not on the outcome. For example, a parent may say, "I can see you worked hard on that piece of homework," crediting the effort the child made. Or, the parent might say, "How does it feel to have that project done?" Encouragement supports independence and motivates exploration.

On the other hand, praise sets up an expectation that raises a child's anxiety level, since the praise may not match up with the child's own self-image. If the parent says, "This is going to be the best in the class," or "You should get an A for this," the child may feel competitive, and thus fearful and less loved. To teach humility, Mother Mary would not have offered Jesus praise, nor would she have spoken judgmental words about his actions. She would have simply encouraged him to do his best.

Help Them Follow Their Hearts

Mother Mary taught Jesus to seek joy, hence his belief that God's will for us is to "rejoice always, pray without ceasing and in everything give thanks" (1 Thessalonians 5:16–18). Jesus was encouraged to find the good in all things, including the Light Within himself and others, and to do that, you have to follow your heart.

Did you know that the heart generates an electromagnetic field sixty times greater than the brain's? Scientists are discovering that our hearts are our navigational systems in this world. They have long been recognized as the center of our feelings and are meant to lead us where God intends for us to go. They connect us with others and they are the source of our joy.

So, ask your kids, "Does this make you happy? If not, let's find out what does!" Teaching kids to follow their hearts leads them to develop their intuition, which helps them make better choices and recognize the opportunities that God presents to them along the way.

Trust in God

Mother Mary had complete trust in God, and you can say, "Well, sure! She had *angels* appearing before her!" But if we can find that trust within ourselves, even without seeing angels, we will be blessed with the removal of all fear. Wouldn't that be a joy?

Trusting in God fills us with a sense of abundance, and that is the best antidote to fear. With God there is never a lack of resources or opportunities. With God there comes unconditional love and the loss of all fear. With the awareness of His presence, we can remember that He has provided our children with amazing gifts, and He will be sure they have the opportunities to develop those gifts and use the light within them to fulfill their purpose on earth. He wants them to shine, and He is there to help them!

Having that trust, that God is with you and on your side, provides greater luxury than any penthouse apartment ever could. It's the luxury of knowing you can do your best and relax inside, knowing that you and your child aren't struggling on alone, but, in truth, walk hand-in-hand with the Divine and have His unlimited love and support.

• • •

These are just a few of the many lessons I've learned from Mother Mary. Jesus didn't have any of the material advantages we give our children today—no electronic gadgets, no sports teams, no energy drinks— yet he was able to become the One whom God created him to be. He was empowered to discover the gifts God had given him without fear of judgment. And a lot of that empowerment came through the unconditional love his mother had for him.

We can help our children become amazingly bright, healthy, and positively influential people if we keep our focus on the Light Within them, as Mother Mary did with Jesus. Dark as these times sometimes seem, there's no less unconditional love available to us today than there was more than two thousand years ago. It resides in our hearts, and in our connection with Mary and her Son, and his Father in Heaven. Let's use that most profound power to help our kids truly succeed and live more heavenly lives, right here on earth.

*Tracey Souverein is the mother of three boys and lives with them and her husband in Fort Collins, Colorado. She has served as a youth minister, a social worker, a community volunteer and a religious education teacher. Her background in human development and family studies helped fuel her interest in parenting techniques, but it has been the amazing guidance from both Jesus and Mother Mary that has directed her to sharing with the world the unique, powerful, and loving ways of parenting at www.WhatWouldMotherMaryDo.com.*

Chapter 17

How to Love Others
Without Losing Yourself

Angela Romero

I f you won't do it for yourself, Lallie, please, do it for your
children—because they're next!"

This was my desperate plea to my dear friend as we sat in the
lawyer's office. Lallie was biting her lower lip as she contemplated
signing the divorce papers before her. She knew she should sign them
and protect herself and her children from her violent husband. But I
knew she was thinking, *How can I?* Divorce represented everything that
was unacceptable to her and her proud Mexican-immigrant parents.
After all, her mom had stood by her father through his addiction and
eventual sobriety.

We'd become fast friends in college in the '90s. I so admired Lallie—
she was strong, independent, and ready to take on the world. I felt she
was the sister I'd never had. My dad died when I was eleven, and I never
met my mother. My dad had always told me she was dead, but before he
died, he confessed she wasn't: She'd just been too young to be a mom.

We didn't meet until I was an adult, so I managed on my own (thanks to those who helped me along the way), as did my older brother. But I felt like I didn't belong anywhere all through my teens.

So it was heaven for me when Lallie invited me into her family for holidays, birthdays, and Sunday dinners. I loved feeling that I was part of her family and that we belonged together. I stood beside her at her wedding and she at mine, and eventually we both had children, jobs, and busy lives. I shared her pain when she suffered a miscarriage, and we shared each other's joy with the births of our sons. She now had three and I had one.

Sadly, I was never fond of her husband, Jerry. He was manic, and his erratic behavior worried me. In the early days he made her happy, but, as the next ten years passed, it became clear that that was no longer the case. Nonetheless, Lallie stood by her man, and I supported her. For one thing, I knew Jerry was jealous of our relationship, and I was afraid he'd force her to choose between us if I opposed him in any way. I was anxious at the thought of losing her.

Time passed and they seemed to be doing all right, but a few years later there was a turning point. I had moved away from California, so we flew out to meet Lallie and Jerry to celebrate Lallie's fortieth birthday, a milestone for us too, marking twenty-one years of friendship. After supper, the husbands went off to gamble, and we went to a concert being held there. On the way, Lallie confided to me that she and Jerry were going through a rough patch, so I wasn't surprised to see tears falling down her face during the concert. I held her hand and my heart ached for her.

Afterward, we learned that Jerry had started a physical fight with my husband over my relationship with Lallie. Chester was okay, but I was afraid: Would Lallie have to choose Jerry over me? Instead, she immediately turned to me and pleaded, "No matter what, we will always be friends, okay, Angie?"

With tears welling up, I nodded and held both her hands tight. I was so glad she felt that way—but I was also realizing something was very wrong. Jerry seemed to be losing control.

Eight months later, I got the call I had been dreading. It was Lallie's sister Selena, asking if I knew where Lallie was. My heart seemed to stop. I realized I hadn't heard from her that week. We immediately started calling everyone Lallie knew and discovered that her three children, ages two, four, and seven, were missing too. No one knew anything about their whereabouts, and the police said they couldn't help until they'd been missing longer. Selena and I were frantic, but we just had to wait. My stomach was in knots and I couldn't eat or sleep.

The next day, Lallie finally called Selena. She said she and the children had been in hiding because she knew they were in danger. Jerry had beaten her, but then he had been arrested for domestic violence, so she and the kids were safe—or so she thought.

Riding on a surge of adrenaline, I booked the first flight out to be with her. I left my two-year-old son for a week and dropped everything. I was a mother and a wife with my own business to run, but I was desperate to help her. I felt I couldn't do anything else.

When I arrived, Lallie and I embraced for a long time, and then she told me what had happened the previous week. Jerry had become enraged as they were talking in bed and began to choke her with one hand while pummeling her with the other. When he stopped, Lallie lay frozen in bed, thinking about how to get away from this madman. When daylight came, she convinced Jerry that she had to go to work early. A coworker then took her to the police station, where she filed a police report and a restraining order. The police picked Jerry up that afternoon on a misdemeanor charge for domestic violence and also charged him with a felony count for the crystal meth they found on him. They kept him in jail, but after only two hours, his parents bailed him out, so she took the kids with her into hiding.

Now we were all in serious danger: Lallie had learned the restraining order carried little weight. Feelings of anger and resentment welled up inside of me like a volcano ready to blow. I had lost so many of the people in my life, and I was not going to lose another. So, I continued to take on Lallie's problems as if they were my own, now feeling even more desperate to save her.

During the week I spent with Lallie, we took all the safety measures we could at her home, installing a security alarm and changing the locks and the garage door codes. She didn't want to move as her neighbors said they wanted to look out for her. And she told me it didn't matter anyway. "Angie," she said, "no matter what, he will still find me."

While we laid low, she told me about her life, which had long been fraught with abuse, just as I'd feared. She'd kept these stories pent up for so long, and now, each word made her lighter and stronger. Over the next few days, with each step we took together—making plans for the children's safety and planning for the future—I saw Lallie coming back.

And now we were in the lawyer's office, looking at divorce papers. My final, and most important job, before I had to leave, was to convince Lallie that she and her children deserved to be free from a life of abuse.

"I know you wouldn't do it for yourself," I said, "but, Lallie, you know you couldn't bear it if anything happened to the kids."

She signed the papers. But she still had a long road to walk to create a new life, free from suffering. After I returned home, we talked almost daily. My life remained on the back burner as I took on everything I could for her—helping her manage her finances and giving emotional support and advice.

Then I learned I was pregnant. I knew I needed to take a step back and slow down to care for my body, my family, and the baby growing inside of me. But Lallie's troubles still pulled me.

And Jerry didn't give up easily. He stalked Lallie when she left work, and she lived in fear. I begged her to tell the police, but she was afraid of Jerry's anger. She made me promise not to report his behavior or his violations of the restraining order, and I complied. It was like helplessly watching a train wreck. I called her attorney and told him I feared for Lallie's safety. I wrote Lallie long emails outlining safety plans, and we talked for hours every day as I helped her make the simplest and toughest decisions.

My stress level continued to mount and, very sadly, I lost the baby at twelve weeks. I curled up in my bed in the fetal position with an overwhelming sorrow and sense of loss. All I could do was lie there and cry, thinking that I had no control over anything.

On a Saturday morning a few months later, I was in the kitchen when the phone rang. It was Lallie's sister, Selena. She asked if Chester was home. My heart raced. I knew. I cried, "Please, tell me Lallie's okay!"

Chester took the phone, and I slid to the floor in a heap, sobbing. I heard him say, "Oh, my God. No."

Lallie was dead. Jerry had entered the house that Saturday morning and choked and stabbed her to death. Jerry was arrested later that day.

My husband and son came with me to California for the funeral, and we stayed to make sure Lallie's boys were taken care of. With all the sadness and the hectic schedule, my body was as stressed as ever. I wasn't sleeping or eating, I was on autopilot, just going, going, going, so I wouldn't have to think about losing Lallie. And then, I learned I was pregnant again. And then, again, to my horror, I miscarried.

Finally, I woke up. Finally, I realized that I failed everyone when I failed myself. Finally, I saw that I mattered too; my life was also precious, and my baby's, and we needed care and attention too.

It was long past time for a change, but I was given another chance. I became pregnant a third time, only two weeks after the last miscarriage, and I devoted myself to keeping this baby alive. I began to read everything I could find about the body's response to stress and what helps to alleviate it. Once I realized the damage that needed to be repaired, I set up a routine to heal my body, mind, and emotions, and over time, thank God, it worked. I gave birth to a healthy baby boy, while his big brother was standing by to welcome him home.

Here are the three main things I started doing to heal myself, and have continued to do every day since:

1. *Just breathe.* I realized that I tend to take shallow breaths when I'm stressed, so I consciously inhale deep, cleansing breaths that reach all the way into my diaphragm. Focusing on my breath helps me relax and puts me into a comfortable space that reduces the stress level. It also clears my mind and allows me to get in touch with my inner self and get directions on what my mind, body, and soul really need at that moment. I've made the huge discovery that when I go within and get very centered within myself, I can find strength and solace, and stay strong for those I love—and for myself.

2. *Ask for help.* Once I've relaxed enough to be able to think about an issue, I break it down to its simplest parts. Then I handle each component of the issue, one by one, giving each the time and attention it needs. This helps me put the issue into perspective. I also ask myself: *Is this a big problem or a little problem? Can I handle this on my own or do I need help, advice, or resources, like counselors, religious leaders, or community programs?*

   Then I ask others for ideas, search the web, read books on the problem, consult my higher power, and learn from others' experiences. I've learned not to be embarrassed to ask for help or to admit to having a problem. What a breakthrough! This also helps me be in the present moment, and keeps my mind from spinning out of control, worrying about the future. A great stress reducer for me is to stay in the moment and put my attention on that moment alone, setting everything else aside.

3. ***Accept what you can't change.*** I ask myself the following questions about the source of my stress: *Is there anything I can do to change this situation, or must I simply accept it for what it is? Can I effect change in this situation, or would acceptance be the better course?*

The trick is knowing the difference. There are times when I just have to accept what I cannot change. I've come to see that if I have an issue with something that's outside of my control, I tend to make it my problem anyway. As I learn to accept what I cannot change, I'm more able move forward and stop dwelling on the issue. Acceptance provides me with a certain serenity and peace within. It helps me to stay positive and let go of the negative, whether by looking at the bright side or at the lessons I'm learning from what I cannot change.

I've also built a strong support system of people and groups around me. I regularly consult my support system in times of need. And I ask myself, *Am I blaming myself (or someone else) for a situation, and do I need to forgive myself (or someone else)?* I have found that blame and anger don't solve problems—what works is taking assertive action to change the things I can, and having the strength to accept the things I can't.

Eight years have passed, and I still practice these stress-reducing steps almost daily. I'm stronger and healthier and much more aware of when I'm overextending myself. I don't often get stressed anymore.

In the end, Jerry pleaded guilty to second degree murder and was sentenced to sixteen years to life with the possibility of parole after ten years. As I write this, Lallie's boys are happy and well-adjusted at ages ten, twelve, and fifteen. They were adopted by Lallie's brother and sister-in-law and now have happy relationships with their three older step-siblings.

We often travel to be with Lallie's boys and her family. I delight in sharing stories of their mom and me with them all. Our children are friends and enjoy joint vacations and birthday parties, as they would have had Lallie lived. Sadly, my marriage didn't survive the severe tests put to it, but my boys make my life full and happy.

I continue to keep Lallie alive in my heart and choose to remember the happy times. I'm grateful for the profound lesson she helped me learn: I can be there for others, but I must take care of myself first, keeping balanced and setting boundaries, so I don't end up with nothing to give. Finally, I have discovered my own self-worth. Now I know that caring for others must begin with caring for myself.

Angela Romero was raised by her single father with her older brother, moving frequently and eventually living off the grid in a rural location until her father developed the area. The whereabouts of her mother were unknown. After her father passed in a tragic accident, she lived independently until moving to be near relatives in Hollywood, California. After earning a bachelor's degree in mass communication, she worked in the health insurance industry and earned her MBA from the University of New Mexico, then started her own employee benefits brokerage in 2002.

Angela lives in Albuquerque, New Mexico, with her two young sons. She surrounds herself with friends and family, including the mother and siblings she never knew as a child. Her mission is to help others maintain a connection with their deceased loved ones through her messages of faith and hope. Angela invites you to visit her website, www.FromLossToFound.com.

Chapter 18

Make the Best of the Bumps on the Road

Lance Rennka

As you've been tooling along on the road of life, have you hit some bumps here and there? We all have our ups and downs; that's for sure. How radical have yours been? Mine have been fairly spectacular. But even if yours have been less catastrophic, I'll bet you'd like to be able to navigate the ones that lie ahead more easily.

If so, here's my question for you: Would you be willing to step back and get a different perspective on your life if it would explain why these bumps happened to you and how you can get the most out of them? I promise you, if you are willing to do that, your life will take off like you won't believe.

Let me start by telling you my story. It begins in Puerto Rico. I had the perfect job—for me. So perfect I couldn't wait to go to work, and I didn't want to go home. I was the dive director of the largest and most sophisticated underwater habitat in the world. Throughout the year, we had five scientists and technicians working in 55–106 feet of turquoise ocean for two weeks at a stretch, carrying out scientific experiments. My number-one job: Keep the aquanauts alive.

I worked seven days a week in a tropical paradise, either underwater or above. Being down in the deep blue sea was heaven to me, and back on dry ground, the palm trees rustled in the eighty-degree breeze, washed by eighty-degree raindrops, while gentle waves lapped at the beach. I was happily married with three young sons, and the uniform of the day was a swimsuit and flip-flops. I may have been the happiest man alive.

Then, one day at work, a line-handling accident broke my arm just above the wrist. Things went south fast. Medical malpractice resulted in a mid-upper-arm amputation during which a suture came off an artery and I bled to death. I was leaning up against the wall in the emergency room, listening to the heart and breathing monitors beeping— then the beeping stopped. I watched the medical team fill my dead body back up with blood and get ready to jump-start me. I drifted up to the ceiling, looked down at my body and said, "Let it go. It's better over here."

I guess the technician didn't hear me. He said, "Clear" and everyone stepped back. He placed the paddles on my chest, my body arched and I dropped back down into it. Next thing I knew I was waking up back in my room.

No, I didn't see the light—only 5 percent of people who've had a near death experience do. But I was certainly changed. To go from the perfect job to death and back to life again is a pretty big bump in the road. But, as I saw it, the bigger bump was to have to live life as a "cripple." My new limitations directly affected my ego, including my self-confidence, self-esteem, and sense of self-worth. I had been a doer all my life—my *job* was problem solving—so while waiting to leave the hospital, I started the questions: "How am I going to tie my shoes, cut a steak, clip my fingernails, do mechanical work, scuba dive, fly a plane, drive a car, perform in bed?" And a myriad of other things I had taken for granted. How was my wife going to view me now? How were my sons going to follow in my footsteps now that I was "hand-decapped"?

To my surprise, by the time I was released from the hospital, I had figured out how to handle most of the requirements of daily life. The next question was, how could I keep my perfect job? To tackle this one head-on, I went back to work the day I was released from the hospital.

I did pretty well, but big bumps kept coming. When I was anesthetized for the skin graft to cover the end of the stump, I found myself outside my body again. This time I'd seriously had enough, so I tried to gain entry to what was behind the Pearly Gates—but I was turned back. The day the stitches were removed, I went back in the water and continued to run the project. Again, I did pretty well. But when the nerves in the stump regenerated, bumping it caused such serious pain that I had to quit my perfect job to have a "stump revision," in effect, a second amputation. And, again, when I was anesthetized, my soul took a trip to the Pearly Gates, and this time it banged on the door for awhile. But they still weren't taking me.

So I spent the next six years proving to myself that I could still do everything I had ever learned to do in order to be productive and earn a living. That included doing most of the trades and being a general contractor and a professional SCUBA instructor trainer and requalifying as a commercial pilot. Then, the fourth of my bumps—a collarbone operation—forced me out of being a general contractor. I had to reinvent myself again, so I did some teaching at a local college and ended up getting a BS degree in industrial technology and a master's degree in education.

All through these years I kept thinking, *Why do there have to be bumps in our lives? What's the point?* And when I asked, *Why me? Here? Now?* and then listened, read, and learned, I started to get the big picture. So here's the lowdown, as I see it.

Prior to birth, our souls, in cooperation with other souls and spiritual entities (including the Cosmic Joker), came into existence for the purpose of evolving and becoming free of the limits of the earth. The plan was to set up the situations, circumstances, relationships, and natural events that would encourage us to use our creative energy and brains to evolve, grow, and, you could say, "wise up."

We were preloaded with a huge database in the form of the DNA we got from our ancestors, including our habits, mental processes, curiosity, survival instincts, ego, and need to be in control. When our soul hooked up to our body/brain, it brought along a footlocker of karmic residue from its past lives to be resolved, which it stowed in our subconscious memory bank. And on top of that we were given free will, making us *able* to change, even though we were predisposed to not want to.

And here's where the bumps come in: They're here to challenge us to make choices beyond our normal, habitual responses to life. From the data we collect as a result of our experiences—including the bumps— we're to determine what works (keep doing that) and what doesn't work (quit doing that). So, whenever we take action, we're supposed to look around and notice: How's that turning out?

Just take a look at your life as you think about this situation. Do you see how you're set up to keep getting the same lessons over and over until you finally understand the changes needed? Look back over your life's journey so far and identify the ups and downs. Now look at the serious bumps, such as injuries, illnesses, accidents, tests of character, financial problems, failed relationships...you name it. These were all exercises to try to get you to learn certain lessons *and change your behavior.* Because behavioral change is the only real way to determine if learning has occurred.

Yes, this life is a seminar, a learning experience, and the bumps along the way are necessary to get us to pay attention. If we fail to pay attention, learn our lessons, and change our behaviors, there will be more bumps further down the road to give us another chance.

But the Cosmic Joker didn't leave us unequipped to take on these challenges. He/She/It gave us a fantastic set of tools we can use to tackle the bumps head-on. I like to call them the Bumps Tool Kit.

The Bumps Tool Kit

When the wiggly connected to the egg, we inherited a set of tools we can use to fix the problems caused by the bumps we experience on our life journey. Here's what's in your Bumps Tool Kit:

- **Survival instinct:** to drive us to find food, clothing, and shelter and to procreate
- **Levels of awareness:** to give us a wide range of levels of consciousness, including nonconscious, unconscious, subconscious, conscious, and super-conscious
- **Curiosity:** to keep us moving forward and evolving
- **Sensory system:** to enable us to gather data from the environment
- **Intuition:** to help us communicate through our soul/mind with the spiritual planes
- **Thinking:** to let us to ask questions, solve problems, and gather new information
- **Learning skills:** to make it possible for us to increase our capabilities
- **Control skills:** to enable us to restrain our emotions, habits, and actions
- **Positive mental attitude:** to help us accept that nothing is an accident
- **Willingness to learn:** to help us accept guidance and grow in wisdom

- **The law of karma:** to show us that there are no punishments or rewards; there are only consequences based on our actions
- **Flexibility:** to give us the willingness to change and take a different route
- **Energy work:** to enable us to draw upon earth energy, cosmic energy, and spiritual energy
- **Creative ability:** to enable us to create through our thoughts, words, and deeds
- **Soul/mind tools:** to let us access our intuition, our prime communications conduit with our spiritual production crew

Yes, you were brought into existence with an extensive set of tools to help you perform your job. And you can and will use all of these tools on your life journey, especially when you're dealing with a bump. Following are the steps I've found most helpful in getting this done.

Seven Steps to Deal with the Bumps in Your Life Journey

1. **Understand the purpose of life.** Life is a seminar. We're supposed to pay attention, learn our lessons, and change our behavior accordingly. There will be tests to ensure we learned the lessons. If we refuse to change, we'll have to repeat the lessons—and the tests.

2. **Be willing to change your beliefs.** My motto is "Question All Beliefs," because our beliefs are often our limitations. We have to put our beliefs to the truth test, including science, reason, gut-check, and intuition from the spirit realm. If they fail one or more of these tests and we keep believing them anyway, bumps will come along to make us think again.

3. **Discover and fulfill your life mission.** A huge part of everyone's life mission is to develop a more positive personality and stronger character traits. We're supposed to *become* someone different,

so we can *do* something different, so we can *have* something different. And this involves gaining knowledge about ourselves and the world, and learning new skills.

4. **Change your perspective about the bumps.** We can do this by accepting responsibility for them as stepping stones to our advancement and remembering that nothing is an accident.

5. **Understand that everyone in your life is a mirror.** Good, bad, or indifferent, everyone in our lives functions as a mirror, so we can see ourselves more clearly and thereby learn and change. So, instead of getting mad, try saying "Thanks." It's truer, and it leaves them scratching their heads!

6. **Learn to love yourself, and discover your passion.** These two goals are what make life worth living. We must be willing to make changes so we can grow to love ourselves—because if we don't love ourselves, we can't love anything, anybody, or God. And discovering our passion and following it brings joy and fulfillment to our lives.

7. **Realize your life purpose.** We are here now, in this time and place, to use our knowledge, skills, talents, and life experiences to serve others and become the best human we can be. This is our destiny. And, oh yeah…it's supposed to be enjoyable!

The bottom line is, it's not the bumps that are important, it's what you tell yourself about the bumps. Learn to listen to the conversations in your head and check to see if you're helping yourself with your attitudes and beliefs, or hurting yourself.

Your job is to use your tool kit and follow the seven steps to deal *effectively* with whatever bumps show up in your life. Maintain a positive mental attitude, pay attention, look for the lessons and change your behavior…and then see if maybe the bumps become fewer as your understanding becomes clearer.

And when the bumps do come, be grateful for them! They're worth way more than a college education. In the big picture, they may be the most valuable part of the ride.

 *Dr. Lance Rennka is an energy worker, a prolific channel writer (spirits write through him), an Advanced Theta practitioner, seminar leader, and trainer. Dr. Rennka's "Brain-On" seminars take us to the next level of data gathering: downloading and sleep-reading directly from the Akashic Record, the Universal Library. The "Soul-On" seminars involve the paranormal modalities, our inherent and inherited capabilities as body/brain–soul/mind dual entities. The "Energy Work" programs develop our capabilities of drawing into our bodies earth energy, cosmic energy, and spiritual energy as we state-shift our brainwave frequencies, which increases our capabilities.*

To learn more about your capabilities, visit www.Lance-Rennka.com.

Chapter 19

Treasure Hunting
for Meaningful Gifts

Lisa Bader

We all know the feeling: A loved one's birthday is coming up and you have absolutely no idea what to get for a gift. I found myself in that situation not long ago, as I looked at the calendar and saw I needed to get gifts for not one, not two, but three friends within the next two weeks. Help!

I hit the mall in search of gifts. As I wandered from store to store, I felt like Goldilocks. This shirt was too big, that one too small; the other was the right size, but definitely the wrong color. On and on it went, as I quickly picked up and dismissed item after item.

Clearly, the problem was that the mall was too small; these sixty-seven stores simply didn't have a sufficient selection! So I moved my search online, and, after hours of surfing through thousands of items, I still couldn't find suitable gifts. And, actually? Even if I had, there was no way I'd be willing to pay the crazy shipping costs. I started thinking about how much time I had spent searching for the birthday gifts and soon targeted the real villains in the story.

Why is he so hard to buy for?! Why is she unwilling to wear any color besides black? What are the odds of having three friends with birthdays within two weeks of each other? Couldn't they have been born during a month that was a little less busy for me?

I eventually did select gifts for the villains...I mean, my friends! But even after all that effort, they were just okay...nothing memorable. I had dinner with a friend a few weeks later and when I mentioned the frustrating hours spent searching, she asked me, "Why do you *have* to get someone a birthday gift?"

I was shocked. Of *course* I had to get birthday gifts! I loved birthdays! These people were important to me and I wanted to find something that each person would enjoy! My friend shrugged and said, "Okay then... you *want* to get someone a birthday gift. So, the gift giving shouldn't be about you. It should be about the person receiving the gift!"

My friend's observation stuck with me, and I started thinking back to the birthdays I had had as a kid. My single-parent and waitress mom always struggled to make ends meet, but she went out of her way to make my sister and me feel like the most special girls in the world on our birthdays. Not that the day was greeted with pomp and circumstance in our house. The signs were much more subtle: The Snoopy birthday mug emerged from the depths of the credenza and was filled with Twizzlers licorice. And then there were a variety of celebrations with family and friends and always, always an ice cream cake that my mom made and served on our official "birthday tray" made of orange plastic...which looked strangely like the trays used at our local burger joint.

How had I shifted from being someone who was thrilled by birthdays to someone who complained about having to buy gifts for the people she loved? When had gift giving become such a production? And did anyone even *like* the gifts I selected? Clearly, it was time to see if I could improve the gift-giving experience for the recipients—and for me.

Put the Joy Back in Giving

Over the next several months, I started shifting my thinking from *having* to get a gift for someone to *wanting* to. Right away, gift giving became a lot more fun and, not surprisingly, the recipients seemed to enjoy the gifts I selected more.

Also, I started paying more attention to gift giving. Over time, I noticed that sometimes a gift that seemed like a winner would be briefly appreciated, while other times a similar item would become a treasured possession. What made the difference? In my search for the "secret sauce," I watched intently as friends exchanged birthday gifts, couples opened wedding gifts, and my own family opened gifts during the holiday season. The sauce clearly had nothing to do with the amount of money spent, or whether the gift was packaged in a brown paper bag or looked like it had come off the cover of a Martha Stewart magazine.

And then at a birthday gathering one day, it hit me. I realized that the gifts that were the most memorable all shared a similar quality: They all reflected the personal connection between the giver and the receiver! Right away, I started putting this insight into action. For a dear friend's birthday, I gave her a special baking spatula and a cookbook of brownie recipes. Though the gift was inexpensive, it underscored our shared love of baking and childhood memories of our moms making brownies that would always stick to the pan.

For my husband's birthday, I celebrated his passion for travel photography by using an online photo site to create melamine dinner plates featuring pictures he had taken on our family vacations. Suddenly, these beautiful images were no longer stored away on a computer hard drive, but part of our family meals on a regular basis.

Go Treasure Hunting for Gifts

Gift by gift, my attitude toward gift giving evolved from it being a tedious item on my to-do list to being one of my favorite activities. Now, I get excited when someone I care about has a birthday or a milestone event because I get to go on a high-stakes treasure hunt! If I'm successful in my search, I find a gift that delights the recipient and shows the person how much I care. If I'm not...well, lives and limbs aren't lost and no child goes hungry. But, I enjoy trying because it's a tremendous opportunity to let someone special in my life know that they are noticed, appreciated, and loved. Plus, it's a wonderful chance to be really creative—something we seem to do less often as adults with grown-up responsibilities.

Following are some of the lessons I've learned while treasure hunting for gifts.

Gift giving is a tangible way to express love and show the receivers you've paid attention to what matters to them

By giving your nephew a book on the Boston Tea Party, you've shown you're aware of his love of colonial America. By giving your mom a "Tea Party for Two" (which might be as simple as a Starbucks gift card and an invitation to join you on a particular day and time), you have recognized that she doesn't really need any more "stuff"; she really just wants to spend time with you.

Any item can be the perfect gift...or the worst gift in the world

A friend of mine received several pairs of socks from her husband on her birthday and was crazy disappointed. Socks?! She wanted something romantic! Another friend *asked* his wife to get him two dozen pairs for his birthday, so he could toss out the old and fill his drawer with nice fresh ones. The perfect gift is in the eye of the beholder!

What matters most is not what's in the box but how what's in the box makes the person *feel*. To me, this is the very essence of gift giving. Though we wrap our gifts in paper and ribbons, you might say they are held together with our emotions. A gift chosen with care can make a person's heart sing; by contrast, a thoughtlessly chosen one can hurt their feelings. A lot. A coworker of mine had a big birthday bash when he turned forty, and when he opened his gifts, he saw that his father had given him a subscription to *Car & Driver* magazine. Ouch! My coworker rode his bike to work and hadn't owned a car in over eight years. He told me later it was a painful reminder of how little his father knew him.

On the other hand, I once sat next to an elderly woman on a plane and was struck by the beautiful mother-of-pearl hair clip that held her mane of gray hair off her face. When I admired it, she told me that her father had given it to her for her sixteenth birthday. He was a very strict, unemotional man, she said, so the idea that he had selected something so lovely had made her feel absolutely beautiful— and still did, all these years later. For better or worse, long after the gift is unwrapped, the memory of the gift can be unwrapped again and again.

Gifts that draw the giver and receiver closer together are the Holy Grail of gift giving

Giving a gift that delights someone? Wonderful! Giving a gift that makes someone feel loved? Awesome! Giving a gift that brings you and the receiver closer? That's the cherry on top of the gift-giving sundae. When the gift not only delights the recipient but also reinforces their relationship with you, it becomes even more powerful. How meaningful when, out of all the people in the world, only you could have given that person that gift.

Here's my litmus test to see whether a gift accomplishes this: If I were to walk into a party and set the birthday gift down among the others, would the recipient know which gift was from me upon opening it? If the answer is "no," I look for ways to make a more personal connection, whether by wrapping the gift in a meaningful way or by including a heartfelt message in the card.

Find Treasures and Enjoy the Hunt

So now, when someone you love is about to celebrate a milestone, *you* get to go on a treasure hunt! (Just picture yourself as a modern-day Indiana Jones.) As any successful adventurer knows, it helps to have a plan to ensure you end up with a great result, so here are some suggestions.

Step 1: Get yourself ready for the treasure hunt

This may seem a bit counterintuitive, but when you need a gift for someone, start by thinking about yourself. What will work for you and make the best possible use of your time? Ask yourself:

- When do you need the gift—tomorrow, next week, next month?
- How much time can you spend searching for a gift?
- How much money do you want to spend on the gift?

Once you've set your boundaries, you're ready to take action.

Step 2: Identify clues to help you find your "treasure" (aka, a highly appreciated gift)

If the recipient has specifically told you what she wants, listen to her! She essentially has told you where the buried treasure is hidden and wants you to dig it up for her.

In the far more likely event that you aren't given this insight, the next step is to really focus on the individual—who she is, what she likes, what's important to her. A few minutes spent answering the following questions can spark some great giving ideas:

- What favorite activity/interest/notable memory do you share?
- What hobbies/interests/recent travels has the person enjoyed?
- What three words would you use to describe the recipient?
- What three words would you *never* use to describe the recipient?
- If the gift could talk, what do you hope it would say?
- What does the recipient appreciate most about gifts? How much care you took, how much money you spent, or something else?

Armed with all of these clues, you are far more likely to give a gift that delights.

Step 3: Make finding your treasure fun and easy

Years ago I had a teacher who said, "If you don't know what you're looking for, how will you know when you've found it?" At the time, he was talking about economics, but the same guidance holds true for gift giving: before you actually start shopping for a gift, or perhaps even making one, it's important to know what you are looking for. You've got some good clues from step 2. To find the actual gift, consider this:

- Does the person have a favorite store or website?
- Do you want to buy, make, or assemble the gift?
- If you only had five minutes to race into the store and grab something, what would it be?

Think about what will make the person smile and about what brought you together and what keeps your relationship going. But don't overthink it! Listen to your gut. And know that sentimental gifts tend to trump all others.

Step 4: Maximize the value of your treasure

Don't you love that wonderful moment when you find a gift you know the recipient will love? Enjoy it! This is the gift you've just given yourself! And, now you can make the gift even more memorable. Here are some suggestions:

- **Include a note that explains *why* you chose that particular gift.** Suddenly, a pair of flip-flops becomes a reminder of a shared memory: "I will never forget how I broke the heel of my shoe at my wedding reception, and you lent me your favorite flip flops. Here's to many more miles of friendship together!"
- **Include something personal as part of the gift.** This doesn't have to be complicated—just something that helps connect you, the recipient, and the gift. If gifting a book, you could include a favorite photo of the two of you to use as a bookmark. If giving a gift certificate to a restaurant, include a menu and circle your favorite dishes.
- **Use creative gift wrapping to highlight something the person enjoys.** Have a friend who loves polka dots? Wrap the gift in polka-dotted wrapping paper or make your own by cutting out circles and gluing to kraft paper. Does the gift recipient love gourmet foods? Tear out some pages from an old cookbook or food magazine, or print out some exotic online recipes and use that to wrap the gift. I promise the person will squeal with delight upon seeing something that was so obviously chosen just for them!

Wrapping It All Up

We all have so many gift-giving occasions every year. Rather than viewing gift giving as a chore or a burden, consider thinking of it as an opportunity to delight someone you care about. When you do, you'll find it makes the gift-giving experience much richer and your relationship even stronger. You might even make a lasting memory in the process—and that's the best treasure of all. Happy hunting!

Lisa Bader is an authority on gift giving and the best-selling author of Wrap with Love: Holiday Gift Giving with Less Stress and More Joy.

She has more than twenty years of experience in operations, branding, and marketing at Procter and Gamble and Intel. As an executive at Intel, Lisa was responsible for developing global in-store and online consumer campaigns. These experiences honed her creative, communications, and problem-solving skills—which, when combined, are the hallmarks of great gift giving.

Lisa has helped tens of thousands of people give great gifts to their loved ones and advanced her mission to put joy back into gift giving. She lives in Northern California with her husband and two children. Check out more of Lisa's gift-giving ideas at www.WrapwithLove.com and at www.Facebook.com/wrapwithlovegifts.

Chapter 20

Turning Your J-O-B into Your J-O-Y: Transform Your Relationship with Your Boss!

Mindy Mackenzie

I t was about the lowest I've ever felt. I was sitting in my office, wondering how I had gotten to such a miserable place in my life. Nine months earlier, I had moved halfway around the world for what had promised to be a fantastic job. I'd be working for a charismatic CEO in a top global position in a new industry that intrigued me. It was so promising that I hadn't hesitated to leave behind a life I loved and a great job at a terrific company working for the best boss I had ever had.

I sat at my desk, my head in my hands, thinking, *Why in the world did I ever leave and take this job? How could I have been so foolish?!?*

It was the first time in my career of twenty-plus years that I had felt significantly unhappy at work. In fact, I dreaded going in to the office. My life outside of work had fallen apart too: I had gained weight, I was overworking and not playing or having any fun, and I was on the road so much I hadn't really connected with anyone in the community where I now lived. But at the heart of my unhappiness was the fact that I was completely out of sync with my boss.

We just could not seem to connect. I had had difficult, challenging bosses before, but this was the most frustrating situation ever. I was working longer and harder, trying to figure out what I was doing wrong. I was never getting off the mobile device and always afraid I was screwing up because he never seemed satisfied with anything I did.

He didn't listen to me, and I felt belittled. Minimized. Disconnected. And what worried me most—I felt increasingly angry. This was a shock because I had always prided myself on how well I worked with my bosses. For most of my career I had loved going to work, but now I was the person going home and complaining. About the boss. About how much my life sucked. How I should have never moved. How miserable I was. How crazy he was.

And I hated myself for it.

When I was growing up, my father would come home every day and complain. He had an endless litany of grievances about the company, his boss, and his coworkers. Everything wrong was always someone else's fault. I remember thinking to myself when I was eight or nine years old that I was never going to be like that. And now I felt like I had turned into my father.

Ouch.

A few days later I was having my monthly telephone call with my mentor/coach. As usual, he asked me how I was doing, so I launched into my diatribe about how stressed out I was and my boss was a complete nightmare and I was thinking about quitting.

After listening to me vent, he said the most profound and simple thing: "Mindy, your boss is not going to change. The only way to get back in control of your life is for *you* to change."

"But I'm not the problem," I retorted. "My boss is. Why should I have to be the one to change???"

"Do you want to be happy or do you want to quit?" he asked.

Well, let me tell you, it pissed me off even to think about quitting. I wasn't a quitter, and I was infuriated at my boss for putting me in the position of even having to consider it. So, I determined right then and there that my mentor was right. I needed to radically change what I was doing, so that I could regain my sense of satisfaction, enjoy going to work, and get happy in my life again.

Over the next year I focused on changing my attitude, my mindset, and my behavior to transform my relationship with my boss. My goal was to subtly lead my boss to interact with me differently by giving myself a mental makeover. In the process of doing so, I came up with the following three principles.

Principle 1: It's All about Your Boss—Not You

This principle is one of the toughest concepts to accept, but it's the most powerful. The first tenet is to acknowledge that it's more about them then it is about you.

Why? Because they have a bigger job. They're accountable for more. They have more pressure. More people to manage. More priorities. More. More. More.

Now, this is probably where you snort derisively to yourself as you think of your own schmucky boss. But if you've ever been promoted into your boss's role, you know how hard the job you minimized actually is. I'll bet that no matter how you felt about your former boss (hero or villain or somewhere in between), you now had at least a smidgen of empathy and respect for him or her. Because *your* life just got harder.

Now, *you* were accountable for more. Had more pressure. More people to manage. More priorities. More. More. More.

This happened to me years ago when I took over as the chief human resources officer for a global $3 billion business. I'll never forget sitting in my office late at night after one month on the job, feeling horrified by my former self and how I had minimized the scale and difficulty of the same role at my previous company. When I had sat in meetings with this executive, there were times when I arrogantly thought, *I could do this job. It's not that hard.* I had never truly appreciated the complexity of the job, the multitude of stakeholders to manage, and the sheer scale and pressure of the global role.

So *why* is it beneficial to you to keep this principle in mind? Because it creates a humbler mindset. It creates a more balanced perspective. It also softens your heart and your hard edge of judgment and makes you more effective.

A highly successful senior executive recently told me a story about how he stopped by his boss's office at the end of a day he knew had been particularly challenging for the man. Earlier that day they had both sat through an hours-long meeting that was incredibly stressful. The boss had been the focal point of a lot of pressure and at one point just "lost it," which he rarely did.

So, this executive swung by his office simply to check in and see how the boss was feeling. As he stuck his head around the corner of the boss's office, he said, "Hey, just doing a mental health check on my way out. I know it's been a tough day. Anything you need?" And then he shut up and listened.

He told me how tensely his boss had been sitting at his desk and how his shoulders dropped in relief. Then he got up and plopped down on his couch and just vented for ten minutes. They both knew there was nothing the executive could do to solve the problem, but that wasn't the point. He had a mindset of "It's about him, not me," and he came from a place of genuine caring, not political gain or ass-kissing. And the boss was grateful for the opportunity just to be heard by someone who cared.

Because that's the thing about this first principle: It only works if you're sincere. If you're faking it, and it's still all about you and your own advancement, that will shine through. Most professionals I've encountered know precisely when their rear end is being kissed (even in the midst of enjoying the smooch-fest), and it doesn't usually help either of you very much.

Principle 1 means getting your focus and attention off of yourself and your needs and focusing on the person you report to. And here's the great thing: The more other-oriented you are, the more likely you are to get your own needs met too. That's just how life works.

Principle 2: Be the Follower You Want
Those Who Report to You to Be

Imagine for a moment if every person who works for you got up every day and said to themselves, "How can I help [*fill your name in here*] today?"

Imagine that every person who works for you is prepared for every meeting. Never wastes your time. Listens first and then speaks. Brings creative solutions to the problems that are worrying you. Anticipates problems and solves them before you even have to ask them to.

And there's more! They take initiative. They keep you informed. They are mature, open, genuine, honest, and balanced. They keep perspective, have a sense of humor, work hard, and get great results.

Wow! *Your life would be awesome!* Admit it. That's your fantasy, right? That's your boss's fantasy, too.

One of the best ways to demonstrate your potential for leadership is to be the follower you would want the people who report to you to be. To anticipate issues. Be prepared. Bring solutions, not just problems. Tell the truth. Listen to the boss first, then speak. (This is a hard one, I admit, because bosses tend to love the sound of their own voices!)

Again, this gets back to your mindset. If it's about them, not you, your orientation will be to respect their time and act accordingly.

This is definitely not about being perfect or about being a "yes" man or woman. It's about walking the proverbial mile in your boss's shoes and reminding yourself that no matter what you think of your boss, they have ten times more stuff to shovel than you do.

So make it easy on them. Make it easy by anticipating, by being prepared, and by *maximizing every minute you are with them*. It is astonishing to me how thoughtless people can be with their boss's time. They treat it as a never-ending reservoir that they are entitled to suck up.

Don't be that person. It's incredibly difficult to lead your boss effectively if you don't treat their time respectfully.

Michael Hall, founder and principal of WildWorks, a highly successfully consultancy based in Sydney, Australia, once advised me to check in with my boss at the beginning or end of every week and ask him, "What is your single greatest priority over the next week?" This simple question would give me the much-needed context for where my boss was coming from and also a broader perspective on the ever-changing dynamics of the business. It would also give me the opportunity to help solve the problems *that mattered most to the CEO*.

Again, ask: "Boss, what is your single greatest priority over the next week?"

When you seek to understand your boss's priorities first, you become the person who takes a broader perspective on the business versus just worrying about your own patch. The person who anticipates. Is prepared. Brings solutions. Is focused on what matters most.

That is the person your boss fantasizes about!

Your boss, in turn, will be much more like the leader *you* fantasize about: someone who listens. Someone who values your opinion, respects your contributions, and trusts you to get the job done.

Principle 3: Challenge Your Boss Effectively

Bosses have egos like anyone does, but with more seniority and larger job titles, these egos tend to expand. As bosses gain more power and influence, those around them tend to manage them more carefully in order to gain favor and more power and influence for themselves. The problem with this repeating pattern is that your boss can get very used to everyone agreeing with him or her and no one truly providing courageous pushback.

At the beginning of my career, when I was seeing clients as a marriage and family therapist, one of the clinical tools I employed was the Stroke-Stroke-Kick method: Provide genuine positive affirmation to the client twice (two strokes) for every time I was going to challenge the client on one of their strongly held beliefs (one kick).

For those of us in the business world, this might sound vaguely like the "sandwich technique" for giving feedback, where you say one positive thing, then insert the negative feedback and then finish on a positive. This is *not* that. When it happens all at once like that, it can come across as flimsy and forced—and everyone knows when it is happening to them.

Effectively employing the Stroke-Stroke-Kick method with your boss means that you are actively looking for genuine opportunities to compliment or affirm him or her. If they give a great speech, tell them. If a certain meeting was handled especially deftly, tell them. If you hear someone else say something positive about them, share it.

The idea is that you are building up a reservoir of genuine goodwill so that when you give them a kick—whether giving constructive feedback, disagreeing on an important issue or challenging a decision—that isn't the only time they're hearing from you. And because both your strokes and your kicks are coming from an honest, authentic place, your boss has a better chance of receiving and responding constructively to your kick.

Remember, if your mindset is that it's all about them, not you, you will want to make it as easy as possible for your boss to respond well to something he or she may not like to hear but, you believe, needs to. And over time, they'll appreciate your input, and even come to rely on it.

• • •

I ended up transforming my relationship with the CEO and working for him happily for almost five years—the longest I had ever worked for someone. In the later years, our relationship could not have been a starker contrast from that first year. We were partners. Collaborators. Mutual challengers. My views were not only listened to and valued but acted upon. I was his "go-to" executive, the one he relied on to fix things or make things happen.

Neither of our personalities had changed. We were both still our unique and crazy selves. But I was happy and loved going to work and making a difference, and my boss made it clear to all that I was one of the highest performers he had ever had.

No matter what your relationship is with your boss right now, you can improve it dramatically by (1) remembering that it's about them, not you, (2) being the follower you want those under you to be, and (3) genuinely caring about your boss enough to provide a 2:1 ratio of positive feedback to challenges and debates. Do these three things and, like me, you might be flat-out astonished by how quickly you make the shift from sadly frustrated to deeply fulfilled!

Mindy Mackenzie has more than 20 years of experience driving transformational change through organizational effectiveness at Walmart, Campbell Soup Company and most recently, Beam, Inc. where she served as Chief Performance Officer and was responsible for company-wide strategy, corporate development and human resources globally.

With an authentic and straightforward style, Mindy focuses on helping leaders in organizations realize that there is only one thing they can reliably change or control in their companies – themselves. She is a sought-after speaker at corporations, conferences and among major colleges. Her mission is to help leaders and executives accelerate their personal and professional fulfillment. She is currently writing a four-book leadership series targeted at business professionals desiring to positively transform their impact on the job. To contact Mindy to speak at your group or for her advisory services, you can reach her at www.mindymackenzie.com.

Chapter 21

Dearly Divorcing: Choose Love and Live Happily Ever After

Ann Calderone

T he day I met my husband-to-be it was love at first sight. Not just for me, but for both of us. It was a regular day, nothing out of the ordinary, and just as I was leaving work, my boss introduced me to the man arriving for his last appointment of the day (whom I'll call Bill). We chatted for maybe thirty seconds, but our eyes met, and that was it. I remember telling my boss the very next morning during our planning meeting, "That guy…what's his name? I'm going to marry him."

I wasn't that kind of "wanna-be-married" girl. I never dreamed of my wedding or Prince Charming. I met plenty of men everywhere I went, and I never fantasized about the perfect Valentine's Day. But I knew, beyond any doubt, that the eyes that had met mine the night before contained missing pieces of my soul. Over the next few weeks, we began the awkward human mating ritual of trying to be cool about getting together, and before long, the ring was on my finger.

Over the years, his career blossomed, and I supported him with everything in me. My life was a balance of gratitude for this wonderful, generous man and the glittering successes he was piling up, and trying not to mind that my fledgling career had been put on hold. Mostly, I happily went along for the ride, ever aware that behind every great man is a supportive woman, not realizing that I was slowly losing myself, one business dinner at a time.

Then the babies came, and it was time to settle down. Our jet-set lifestyle started to slow down about the same time we chose to leave the city for the good schools of the suburbs. The perfect home was dropped in our laps, and we jumped right into a new phase of life. But the rocky places in our relationship got rockier after the move. I was doing the mommy thing while Bill was getting busier and traveling away from home more. I thought I could do it all; after all, I was "just" a stay-at-home mom with all the resources I needed. I didn't see anyone else caving into…what were these feelings? I thought I was just missing the mental stimulation of working outside the home. But when the last child's stork made a precarious landing, it all came crashing down.

After a healthy seven months of pregnancy, I went into distress while out of town on a rare trip with Bill and was admitted to the neonatal intensive-care unit. Separated from my boys, who were being cared for by my sisters on the other side of the country, I was filled with anxiety as each new day brought a new worst-case scenario for my unborn child and me. My husband was incredible. Somehow he managed to hold my hand in the mornings, fly across the country to kiss the kids goodnight, and meet with clients somewhere in between. He rocked it—but I didn't. In a constant state of panic, I became more and more anxious in the final harrowing weeks of the pregnancy.

Miraculously, our third son was born on time, healthy and beautiful. I, however, remained an emotional wreck, and soon after I arrived home from the hospital, depression set in. Only, I didn't know it, because everything looked the same: Bill was still working and traveling, and I had a new baby and a couple of toddlers to deal with. But the days drifted away in dark clouds, and the nights were unbearable for me. I was trying to eat and sleep and train the little ones to do likewise, while Bill caught yet another red-eye and went straight to the office. I couldn't blame him—he got more sleep in business class than he ever would have at home—but the tolls of resentment and fatigue were adding up.

Despite our strong beginning, the subsequent ten years together had been full of ups and downs, with the ups becoming fewer each year. With a new baby, we had a new reason to bolster our commitment, so we hung in there, keeping the family stable for its newest member and seeing if he might work some magic. But after a year and a half had passed, we realized we were kidding ourselves and we couldn't go on as we were. And so we separated. Bill packed his things and moved out, and I basically climbed into bed for, oh, a few months or so.

I felt worse than ever because now there was more loneliness and isolation, the feeling I'd failed, the weight of managing the house and kids on my own, and, I'll admit it, resentment at the idea of the freedom my husband now had in his rented city apartment. I was stuck in a slump for months, despite gradually starting to do things to improve my well-being. I went to therapy, worked out, ate healthier—and Bill, in the city, did too. Eventually, persistence paid off, and the light got brighter. We thought, hoped, *Maybe our trouble was just about depression, fatigue, and the stresses of having a family*, and we kept the idea of reconciliation alive.

But another two years passed and it was clear to both of us that our issues went deeper than any of that. We had great chemistry, but we were happier apart. And we finally figured out that we'd have the best chance of staying united in our mission to be good parents if we stayed separated. Although we had intended to be together till death did us part, we realized that, for us, the only reward in staying together that long would be, well…death! While it was heartbreaking to wake up day after day with the thought that this wasn't how it was supposed to turn out, we decided that the next best thing to a happy marriage would be an amicable divorce. We knew this was a hard thing to achieve, but we became determined to pull it off.

It wasn't easy to divide up the life we'd built together, but somewhere in the midst of all those details, an "a-ha moment" came and set me on a path that changed my life forever. I'd like to share my experience to show you that it *is* humanly possible to have a positive breakup, in spite of the pain.

As my marriage dissolved, I received a lot of calls and mail from well-meaning friends and relatives with advice, prayers, even Mass cards with the single intention that Bill and I stay together. But the end of our marriage wasn't something horrible. It was just a difficult reality we had to accept: The relationship we had once had was gone. And, after some real soul-searching, I realized that *it was okay that the marriage was ending*. And that acceptance and honest assessment, without assigning any blame, was the silver lining of my divorce.

Of course, we'd never wanted our children to have to go through this. But we knew that for them to grow up happy, they had to have reasonably happy parents. And, it's hard to be happy when you're with someone who doesn't inspire your best. In our case, we had once been perfect partners, but our paths were diverging and we could no longer create the happy home together that our boys deserved. While it was more frightening to separate than to stay together, we could no longer ignore the next step. Luckily, that didn't mean there had to be hard feelings. Here's how we managed to stay sane and reasonably friendly through it all.

Five Keys to Dearly Divorcing

1. Reach out to friends

This is the hardest thing to do sometimes, but this is exactly what friends are for. These are the people who can love you when you feel your worst. *And they do.* My brother used to say, "People love to help, so let them."

When I crawled into bed after Bill moved out, my girlfriends kept calling to offer support. Foolishly, I tried to keep everybody at bay because I didn't want them to see my weakness. Fortunately, I have a wonderful friend (and so do you—there's at least one in every life!) who came over one day and wouldn't take no for an answer. She looked at me and said: "No more. You've been wearing that sweatshirt for a week. It's time to shower!" She helped me put an outfit together and took me shopping for two more to accommodate the lost baby weight, so that I could be presentable on the days I was too stubborn to accept help.

This one act of kindness saved me; it allowed me to look in the mirror and see that I was human and I had something to offer, and, also, I had more I could give my kids! This isn't only true for women; Bill told me years later that he knew who his true friends were the night they showed up and took him to a local pub and spent the entire evening wordlessly watching the game that was on TV, just to let him know they cared—in that manly sort of way. After that, he was able to open up with them about what was happening, and his friendships became stronger.

2. Recognize the person you married inside the person you're divorcing

During the worst days, I hated my husband and blamed him for moving out, even though it was the most practical arrangement. Nonetheless, the most valuable thing I did during this painful time was embrace love. One day while rocking the baby, I remembered that there was a reason I had married this man: He was a good man! We had had some great years together, and he had given me three wonderful children. It wasn't an I-win-you-lose competition; it was a mutually painful separation. Could I allow him to be who he is now and love him for his courage to grow—even if it was away from me? Of course I could, because our history was one of love. I would still love him, even if I couldn't live with him. The love from our traditional history would be the foundation for our unconventional future.

3. Rephrase it

Divorce isn't a failure; it's a signal that a new chapter is beginning. Instead of saying our marriage failed, we noted our three beautiful children and called it a smashing success! In response to everyone who was "pulling for us to make it," we got together and wrote a "press release" explaining that our marriage was a successful joint venture that had run its course, like *Seinfeld*. It was easier to understand when we compared our union to a carton of milk: It was fresh for a time, but the expiration date was upon us, and we had decided to finish it off before it spoiled. This was helpful because, by reframing what people thought was a tragedy as a natural occurrence, we were able to focus on the good we had experienced together and not dwell on the pain.

4. Remember, your ex will always be a part of the fabric of your life, so try not to stain it!

Divorce can be messy. There are so many things to consider regarding financial and custody concerns if there are children involved, and these are serious issues. Emotions can get the best of us while we try to do the practical and manage the emotional.

When Bill and I began to discuss the details of divorce, we knew that this was where it could get destructive. We'd heard only horror stories, so we went to see a mediator. We didn't want our family to be ripped apart; we simply wanted to pursue our individual paths. In that spirit, we put away our fear of "not having enough" and our need to "win at all cost" during the proceedings and, instead, trusted each other to be honorable and focused on what we wanted our family to look like at, say, our first son's graduation from college. Would I really want an alimony dispute to smudge the happy faces in that photo? Did I want my marriage to be a waste of all those years, or a deposit into the bank of love and wisdom? There were good memories to honor, and, while the process wasn't always fun, we came away with less anxiety and animosity than we started with. We knew we'd always have a common bond in our children, and it made so much more sense for them to have an "unconventional" but loving family, rather than a "broken" and unhappy one.

5. Let go

You might prefer to say, "Give it up to God," or "Release it to the universe." Some people might argue that they can't let go of whatever led to the divorce. But you must decide: Do you really want to suffer through your separation and forever after? Or do you want to grow in courage and strength and move on peacefully? If you don't like the phrase "Let go," try this one: "Trust." Not in your ex necessarily, especially if it was a breach of trust that got you reading this! But trust in yourself and in that Something that's bigger than you. Can you trust yourself to grow from this experience? Can you trust a higher power, the universe, God, angels, or whatever you believe in, to see you through this challenge?

When I went through the hardest part of the separation—the holiday season that first year—I kept repeating: "Trust, let go, and believe it's all good." It was my mantra, even when I didn't really believe it. Then, one day, I found myself in New York City and, lo and behold, Macy's had strung up their Christmas lights with one word across the entire façade of the building: *Believe.* It still gives me goose bumps when I remember how my prayers were answered in a simple word for all the world to see, and the message has never left me. From that moment on, through challenges and triumphs, I've known one thing: I trust and believe that all things are ultimately for a higher good.

• • •

So, if you're facing a separation or a divorce, look for the silver lining—which is, simply, love. Love opened my eyes to better see where I was in my life, where I wanted to go, and what I wanted for my children. Use these five keys with love in your heart, and your chapter on divorce can also have a happy ending.

Ann Calderone is a stay-at-home mother of three boys and a devoted partner to her former husband in creating a harmoniously unconventional family. She spent many years working in talk and sports radio, in Washington, DC, and New York City, with top personalities, including Larry King. She's also a private pilot.

Wishing to provide support for underserved populations, Ann joined forces with other moms to form Project Neighbor, an organization that matched local families with volunteers to assist them with specific challenges. She also served as chairperson of her local Community Service Committee, which received numerous awards during her tenure for its unique approach to bringing community and global awareness and service to young children.

Ann's essay about her prom date was published in Bethesda Magazine, and she's currently writing a book about divorce. She would love for you share your divorce experience at www.DearlyDivorcing.com.

Chapter 22

Will He Call Me? Break Your Addiction to Unavailable Men!

Sarah Kotz

I *'ll never be treated that way again!* That's what I promised myself after I came out of a toxic five-year relationship a few years ago.

But it was hard: My self-esteem was mangled, and I was only just starting to tap into who I truly was in my twenties. I became a "serial dater" for a few years, dating new guys all the time. I just wasn't meeting Mr. Right, and I was discouraged in love and life, to say the least.

I felt sad that the only thing seemingly missing in my life was the "ultimate man." I had the career I'd always wanted, and everything seemed perfect except for this one thing: *the relationship*. I tried online dating and meeting guys through friends or by going to bars or the gym…the usual. Men were popping into my life, but they never seemed to work out.

I started to see a pattern in my life and my friends' lives of dating what I called "the Unavailable Man."

I met one of my unavailable men (I'll call him Bryan) on a dating site. The moment Bryan walked up on that first date, I was super attracted to him: He was the epitome of tall, dark, and handsome. We immediately hit it off and talked for hours on our first date, and by date three, I was really starting to let my guard down.

Then, I stopped hearing from him. I always became obsessed with finding out why when that happened, so I reached out to him, breaking the conventional world's rules, and asked him if anything was wrong. Bryan said he felt that I wanted a relationship, and he couldn't deliver on that, but he still wanted to be in touch.

You would think I would walk away at this point, but no. What did I do? I decided I was going to convince him that he *was* ready for a relationship! So I continued to reach out, while still playing the "cool-girl card," showing that I didn't care that he had backed off, and I didn't mind only talking to him when he wanted to. But eventually Bryan just stopped reaching out or responding, and I felt worthless—and at the same time desperate for him to know how great I was! I honestly felt like I should be in an insane asylum.

But I know I'm not alone. Women feel hurt and confused all the time by men who don't want a relationship. It's so hard to accept that they truly are Unavailable Men!

The red flags I didn't take seriously were:

- He told me he didn't want a relationship!
- The communication was always on his terms.
- He would disappear and/or not respond for days.

The Unavailable Man is everywhere. Let's look at another example.

The Story of Rachel and Dan

Rachel had been at the conference for a few days and had seen many speakers, but then *he* walked on stage. He was different from anyone she had ever laid eyes on: He was dressed in jeans and a blazer, unlike the stiff suits the other speakers were wearing, and he was so handsome. He introduced himself on stage and immediately Rachel was captivated. After the hour-long session, Rachel knew she needed to meet this man, but there were so many people surrounding him that she finally gave up and left, not sure if they'd cross paths again.

It didn't happen till the last day of the conference. Rachel was getting out of the elevator with her bags, and there he was. They immediately made eye contact, but Dan just smiled and kept on walking. Rachel yelled after him in the busy hotel lobby, "Wait! I have questions!!"

Dan turned around with an amused smile on his face. Rachel was flustered but managed to start a chat about business to distract him from her awkwardness. Before they parted, Rachel and Dan exchanged their contact information on the premise that they would be exchanging business ideas—but both knew otherwise.

There's always something so exciting about meeting someone new. Rachel began taking frequent trips to Chicago, where Dan lived, and being with him was wonderful at first. But time passed and Dan still only let her into his life enough to meet her at her hotel and have one or two days and nights of mind-blowing sex and room-service food together. She was never privy to his personal life, his home, or anything else, except for his work—and his body. Each time they met, Rachel had hopes of a different outcome, but she was always disappointed.

By letting this pattern continue, Rachel did herself harm. She saw her sense of self-worth break down, she began to question her sanity and she kept herself in a constant emotional tailspin. But she was in love with Dan and afraid of chasing him away or looking needy, so she refused to speak up about her concerns. She knew there were red flags, but she was so addicted to having *something* with Dan that she brushed them aside.

Here are a few of the many red flags in this example:

- He only makes himself available for short stints of time and often not on weekends or for the entire weekend.
- He doesn't open up about his personal life.
- The relationship with him is predominantly about sex.
- He never shows you where he lives.
- He only talks about himself and hardly asks about your life.

In this example, Rachel had never even asked Dan if he was already in a relationship, or wanted to be in a relationship, for that matter. Being afraid to clarify with a man what his status is, or what he wants, is one of the biggest mistakes a woman can ever make. However afraid you might be that you're going to "mess it up" by asking a man where you stand, you set yourself up for heartbreak the minute you choose not to ask those questions.

If anything, asking those questions early on is an opportunity to make it clear to the man that your time is valuable and your life is precious. If he's not on the same page, you'll find a man who is! *Next!*

Most of the decisions and choices we make when first getting to know a man and choosing whether or not to spend time with him stem from our feelings of self-worth. When we finally take the attention we've been putting on men who treat us badly and put it on activities that will build *ourselves* up, first and foremost, we finally begin to make ourselves available for a healthy, happy relationship.

When we truly "get it" that we are not only "good enough," but actually a beautiful soul who gives, and deserves to receive, the very best in life, we start making different decisions when it comes to men. Our standards change, and we no longer consider a man who wants to use us for sex or pick and choose when he sees us. These are men we immediately walk away from. They are not worth our time of day.

Let's look at one more example.

The Story of Laura and Thomas

When Laura met Thomas for the first time at a party, they were both in a relationship with someone else. Despite this, they talked for hours about anything and everything. When they ran into each other the second time at another party, Laura was single again, and they wound up huddled in the corner, talking intimately. Laura knew Thomas had been in a relationship for some time, but that didn't stop either of them from talking the whole night and exchanging numbers.

This started an intense virtual affair. Laura and Thomas would talk, text, and Skype all day every day. The connection turned sexual virtually, via text and Skype dates, and eventually led to some casual hangouts. It was very tumultuous for Laura because Thomas would often say, "Yeah, we can hang out," and then wouldn't show up. Laura would be left heartbroken and disappointed.

Laura knew the relationship wasn't right, but she was sure it would only be a matter of time before Thomas would leave his girlfriend, and then they could develop their relationship. He clearly liked her a lot! But as days turned to months, Laura realized that this man was not leaving his girlfriend. By this time she was entirely in love, her self-esteem was in shreds and she was bitter about the time she had lost pursuing a relationship with this Unavailable Man.

The red flag with this example is:

- *He's with another woman!!*

• • •

You might be saying, "These women should have known! These are clearly examples of men who are not available." But we all know how hard it can be to defy the attraction and allure of certain people. Thomas had touched Laura's heart, and once she had fallen in love with him, she didn't *want* to pull herself away, despite the continuous rejection.

But pursuing a man who's in a relationship and is willing to cheat is a great big billboard-size sign that he is not ready for another relationship! You have to do yourself a favor and *run*—immediately!

Unfortunately, there can be something intoxicating about that Unavailable Man. But, if you don't want to suffer, you have to be very strong and clear-headed, and recognize him *before you get roped in* and start to love him.

So, how do you recognize an Unavailable Man? Let's review.

Are you experiencing one or more of the following?

- He only makes himself available for short stints, often less than a twenty-four-hour period in a week.
- He doesn't spend time with you on the weekends. Men who are not ready for a relationship tend to see you on a weekday or after hanging out with their buddies on the weekend.
- He doesn't open up about his personal life. He only talks about himself and rarely asks about your life.
- Your relationship is predominantly about sex.
- You've never seen where he lives. He never invites you over.
- He only calls you late at night or when he's drunk.
- He just got out of a relationship—and, if his ex's stuff is still in their old place or he's still texting back and forth with her, he isn't really out of it!
- He's currently in a relationship! (This one should be self-explanatory.)

- He tells you he doesn't want anything serious right now. This one should also be very clear! If he tells you this, *believe him.* It's a huge mistake to refuse to believe a man when he tells you his truth!

From my experience, I know that women are often willing to accept less than they deserve because they're afraid of being alone. We glorify the man we're with, even if he's giving us signs that he isn't the one, and he isn't treating us the way we want to be treated. And, it can get worse if he leaves because then the fantasy thinking starts, and we can begin to blame ourselves and make the relationship seem better than it was.

When self-doubt starts to creep in and you blame yourself for the demise of a relationship, or you just aren't getting what you want out of a relationship, ask yourself the following questions:

- What if letting go of this Unavailable Man meant meeting a wonderful man who was truly and fully available right around the next corner? You'll never know until you stop wasting time with this man!
- What if this bad relationship wasn't your fault and the breakup had nothing to do with you? This man might just not be right for you or ready for you—or anyone!
- What if this had nothing do with another woman? We seem to obsess about not being chosen and wanting to be the chosen one. We have to stop that! This has nothing to do with another woman being better than you.
- What if you are already enough? For the right man, you are *already way more than enough!* You're the best! You could be the prettiest, smartest, funniest woman in the world, but if this guy isn't ready or isn't the one for you, it doesn't matter: He won't

want you! But your looks, your smarts, and everything about you will be perfect for the right man.

- What could you do in this moment to bring *yourself* back to you and make *you* feel good? Nurture yourself. Take a bath, go for a run, meditate, go out with friends, do anything that brings you joy! And cultivate your friendships with girlfriends. When your life is fun and full of love, you won't put up with a man who makes you suffer!

It's important to *always* remember that when relationships don't work out, it's an opportunity for someone even better to come along. We need to learn to trust these moments, and grieve and let go. Letting go is the hardest part. Our instinct can be to try to control the situation, whether by following the person online or trying to convince them that we're the best thing for them.

Instead, take a moment and breathe. Then remind yourself that if this is the right man for you, the best thing you can do is let him go. Let him take all the time he needs to build himself back up or get over someone else, so that he can come back to you as the partner you really want. And if he doesn't come back to you, that's fine! You don't need him. There's a better partner waiting for you around the corner.

What if you could trust that? What if you could believe that you don't have to make anything happen? What if you knew that the right man will come to you if you can just relax, enjoy each day, and not put up with less in the meanwhile? That's what it means to reclaim your power and be ready *yourself* for an Available Man!

Navigating through the minefield we call dating can be extremely difficult. But we can make it easier on ourselves when we recognize the types of relationships we've been attracting and have the confidence in ourselves to walk away when a relationship doesn't serve our happiness and our emotional health.

Believe in yourself! And then watch men start to believe in you too. If you love and respect yourself, men will do the same, and your dating scene will stop being a minefield and start being fun. Then, one day, the ultimate relationship of your dreams will no longer be a childhood fairy tale—the Available Man of your dreams will show up, and it'll be a real-world reality.

Through hard-won personal experience of the current dating scene, Sarah Kotz learned how to overcome self-doubt and ultimately find self-love. She is an advocate and coach for girls and women, helping them move through the journey of finding their perfect partner by first finding their love for themselves.

Sarah has been a passionate writer since the time she could first hold a pen. She has a BA in psychology and a postgraduate degree in human resources management. No longer able to ignore her true passion, Sarah recently left her eight-year tenured corporate management position to pursue her writing career, focusing on dating and relationships. She is currently embracing her single life and living in Toronto.

You can connect with Sarah at www.sarahkotz.com.

Chapter 23

PTSD, Who Me?

Ayo Kenyatta Haynes

W hen did this happen?"

"Twenty-two years ago."

"Oh…are you an alcoholic?"

"No."

"Drug user?"

"No."

"Sexually promiscuous?"

"No."

"Gay?"

"No."

At first I didn't know why this stranger was asking me these questions and why she sounded so incredulous with each "no" I uttered. By the end of our conversation I realized, without help dealing with what happened to me so long ago, by her standards I was a marvel!

Although I was in the midst of an emotional crisis (that I later called my "great depression"), here I stood twenty-two years later and a few months after 9/11, talking on a New York City pay phone to a stranger about something few had ever been privy to. What I had been through was like being shot with a hollow point bullet that explodes inside you. Most of the bullet fragments had been removed, and most of the pain along with it. However, a few fragments remained, and my body was trying to get rid of them, little by little pushing them to the surface so they could be removed.

That's exactly how my psyche dealt with the attempted rape I endured when I was ten years old—slowly pushing the long suppressed issue to the surface but at a controlled speed.

Over the years, I successfully overcame other fears that stemmed from that attack, such as traveling alone. I had taken several solo transatlantic trips that helped me reclaim my adventurous and independent spirit, so I was not expecting the crippling fear that struck me after 9/11. That fear was that the end of the world was immediately eminent.

The events of 9/11 for me were like getting "shot" again in the same spot as I did in 1978. This time my psyche was saying, "*Enough! Deal with this now or else!*" In hindsight, that day was a textbook watershed event that precipitated my post-traumatic stress disorder (PTSD) and set off a chain of unexpected events and emotions I wasn't ready to have surface so quickly—or dramatically. With no way of knowing, for me Tuesday, September 11, 2001, created a wormhole back in time to Thursday, June 1, 1978. For all intents and purposes it was the same day. The events of 9/11 tapped right into the vulnerable space occupied by the long overlooked and painful memory of the brutal attack.

In 2001, PTSD was still that "thing" your uncle who fought in Vietnam had been dealing with all those years since his return. It was usually associated with men, not women, and veterans of war, not civilians. Yet here I stood knee-deep in a disorder I didn't even know I had until many years later.

The experience had been left mostly undisturbed for twenty-two years. A few months after the horrifying event I began to show signs of "acting out," so my mother brought me to a prayer service with the intention to deal with the after-effects of the attack. After the service, I walked out of the church with my mother and felt a lightness I hadn't experienced since the attack, and because I felt and acted better, no one suspected that there were "bullet fragments" that remained.

Talking Can Ease the Pain

Traumatic childhood events such as divorce, injury, physical or sexual abuse, or death of a parent or sibling all have the ability to shut you down. If left unresolved, a later event of similar intensity can reactivate the emotions created by the original trauma. By talking about the trauma and giving it "oxygen," you can alleviate some of the painful effects.

Unfortunately, in my family we didn't talk about what happened to me. So the psychological trauma soon took up dormant but long-term residence. An hour or so after the attempted rape, my best friend from school called me to rehash the day's events as we always did. Just as I was about to recount what had just happened to me, my uncle, who my mother had called to help us, grabbed the phone and covered the receiver. He said I was *never* to tell anyone what happened. And I didn't—for damn near twenty years. My mother never brought it up either, even after the prayer service. I suspect she wanted to protect me from that awful memory, and because I was such a high achiever she didn't think any harm would come from letting sleeping dogs lie.

Choose Whom You Tell!

Clearly, a fellow ten-year-old was not the right person to tell about the attempted rape, and neither was the guy I dated many years later.

After successfully completing several months of professional therapy at the local rape crisis center, I felt liberated, having worked on the many issues of the attack. I knew better than to share so openly with someone I barely knew, but I felt exhilarated on the date and so comfortable with him. I excitedly shared how I was looking forward to being in a new relationship with my new frame of mind. When he asked me why that was, I didn't have a lie ready at hand, so I simply told him the truth.

The more I tried to convince him that I was in a "great space," the more he remained convinced that I was "damaged goods." His experience with women who had similar encounters had clearly colored the lenses through which he viewed me. It was an inappropriate time to share, and we had no relationship history where that kind of information could land right side up.

That date set me back big time in the sharing department. It took years for me to get up the nerve to share my story with a man with whom I was romantically involved. So be discerning with whom you share both your story and your victories, and when you share. You need to be in a relationship of deep mutual trust to share something so tender so that it will be treated with the understanding it deserves. This is especially important if the victory hasn't had a chance to take root at the level the trauma was experienced.

Be Open to Alternative Healing Modalities

As a preteen, the hands-on, all-night prayer service at an evangelical church was nowhere on my radar as a way of healing—but it was for my young, single mother. Today, many people get therapy in the face of a traumatic event. However, in 1978, therapists and psychiatrists were for the rich or eccentric. Even if you had money, talking about your problems with a complete stranger was a no-no. Attending church and seeking out your priest or pastor was very acceptable.

But at thirty-two, in the midst of a major emotional breakdown, church didn't have the same success as it had earlier in my life. I still believed heartily in God, but I was floundering emotionally. By chance, while out with one of the few friends I let know how depressed I was, she noticed a tarot card reader set up in a corner of the restaurant. She wanted a reading and I, with my Christian sensibilities, wanted no part of it. But when she asked me to sit with her during the reading and record what was being said I reluctantly said yes. I was astonished by what I was hearing; the woman was telling my friend about many things we had talked about earlier that night.

Desperate to find the source of my depression, I left my reluctance for tarot card readers and psychics behind, and in the hush-tones and candle light of this space, she asked why I wanted a reading. My answer was simple: "I'm depressed and I don't know why."

Over the course of the twenty-minute reading she told me about a past life, and past events in this life, leaving one card unturned. Turning over that final card and staring at it for along time, she asked: "Were you ever raped or molested as a child?" My tears, pouring forth like Niagara Falls, answered her question. My body has always reacted to hearing and feeling soul truths with tears. When I could finally speak I said, "Yes," and told her what happened to me when I was ten.

"Did you ever get therapy?" she asked.

"No, but my mother took me to an evangelical church where they laid hands on me and delivered me from all of that." It sounded ridiculous to even me, but she replied "I'm sure it did help, and I am glad she brought you there, but that only healed the spiritual part of you," she said. "You still need to deal with the human side of you." The already removed bullet fragments represented the spiritual side of me and the remaining ones, the physical.

So there it was...it was time for the rest of the fragments to be extracted. By some force they were being pushed to the surface to finally be dealt with. This incredibly esoteric woman gave me a most down-to-earth message that led me to seek out traditional psychotherapy. She gave me the number to the rape crisis center. I called first thing the next day, and the rest is my history.

One of the concepts my therapist at the center spent a lot of time working with me on was seeing myself as an actual ten year-old and not a younger version of my current self, which I had a difficult time doing but was crucial in order to heal the human side of me. It would still be many years later before I realized that I had been struggling with overcoming PTSD.

Now, I'm not saying run out and find a psychic to give you a reading, but consider that cultural and familial norms may be holding you back from seeking counseling or other help, and be open to various modalities that can lead to your healing. Perhaps it's studying Kabbalah, practicing kundalini yoga, meditating, studying network spinal analysis, or attending life wellness workshops given by people who have transcended their own issues of abuse, addiction, physical challenge, or depression. Many people ignore the spiritual side of their being—the most crucial part in our healing—and focus wholly on the physical/psychological. Or like me, they focus wholly on the spiritual side and ignore the physical. The only way to fully take back our lives is to heal both our physical and spiritual selves to establish, or reestablish, balance.

Life Doesn't Happen to You, It Happens for You!

After 9/11, I attended an artists' retreat weekend, where I finally shared with strangers what happened to me as a child. Feeling safe and experiencing no judgment in this small group setting, I distinctly remember feeling that I had solved one of the mysteries of the universe as I listened and then shared my story.

I realized in that moment, whatever had happened to me in this lifetime, positive or negative, was something I *chose* before being born—my parents, siblings, where I lived, if I would go to college, etc. Through free will, and greater understanding, out of many possible scenarios, I had chosen which events and circumstances would serve me best for optimal spiritual growth.

Most people would question, or even disagree, that anyone would *choose* to be raped, abused, bullied, in a crippling accident, die young, and so on. From a human standpoint, I would say few outside of spiritual masters or those who are self-aware would agree that they had a choice in which "negative" experiences would occur in their life, and that these events would serve to reconnect and remind them of who they were spiritually.

Once I understood that my soul chose to endure a brutal event because it knew the experience would lead to an incredible breakthrough that would leave me stronger than ever, my healing took off! From that time of realization, I decided that childhood attack would not be my life story. Rather, working through the pain—both physically and spiritually—would allow it to only be a *chapter* in the amazing story of my life!

Too many people allow a traumatic event to consume them, and then need to take great quantities of alcohol, drugs, sex, or food in order to quiet the savage beast within. We all make spiritual agreements with God before being born, knowing our souls can handle the experiences. There were times where the physical and rational part of me forgot or couldn't comprehend that soul agreement, and even my preordained greatness. I thank God I eventually did remember, and I'm determined to help others who are dealing with unbearable pain that has shut them down or knocked them off their life course.

I never understood anyone who contemplated or committed suicide until my own great depression. Although suicide was not something I personally would consider, I understood the deep pain and desperation that got someone to that point. Before my own experience with depression my level of empathy and understanding was nonexistent. The opposite is true now.

Don't Be a Victim Again

Many of us don't know we're playing the game of victimhood. When life "happens" it is easy to get overwhelmed with a "why me?" mentality. Anytime I felt wronged, I had a bad habit of rehashing the event over and over with my extremely patient girlfriends looking for "validation" of the mistreatment I was feeling. I finally broke that habit. Surprisingly, doing that helped me work on forgiving others and moving on rather than staying in the time-wasting, endless loop of blaming others. I didn't realize this constant rehashing and reliving events was a classic symptom of PTSD.

Much like a functioning alcoholic, we are a society that says we're fine when we are not. We insist on "functioning" through pain or suffering rather than dealing with it. If you Google PTSD, millions of sites come up. The Anxiety and Depression Association of America says that 7.7 million people suffer from PTSD. I think it is much, much higher! PTSD research has been primarily based on those in the military (I believe and know that it is expressed differently in civilian life), then victims of sexual attacks, and then victims of physical attack. But to limit PTSD to those three areas is to greatly underestimate the destructive power this disorder can have in the lives of anyone who has experienced any other type of trauma.

To heal from PTSD, it's important to know the symptoms. Reliving the event over and over, emotional avoidance, and an unquiet mind are just a few of the signs. There are many ways individual psyches can deal with the effects of a traumatic event, and that's why I believe it should be called PTSS—post-traumatic stress syndrome. So if you're experiencing any of these symptoms, or something similar, there may be unresolved trauma in your past that you need to deal with right away.

The only way to overcome PTSD is to work through the trauma and heal the pain associated with the event or situation. My path to healing PTSD may be different from yours. If your path leads you to discover, or rediscover, a hidden piece of your soul, then go with it. Allow your spirit to guide you to the right place(s), people, and modalities that remind you the traumatic event is only a chapter in your life's story. You and your complete story are far greater.

Ayo Kenyatta Haynes is the daughter of a Presbyterian minister mother and a jazz musician father. Her life experiences, which include travels around the world, including all 50 States, brought her to the realization that spirituality is paramount to religiosity.

Even before overcoming a childhood trauma, Ayo has always been a champion of the underdog. She lends her voice and spare time to various charities by serving on their Board of Directors.

Ayo holds an MBA, is a Lic. Associate Real Estate Broker and continues a 25 plus year career in acting. Her biggest life joy comes as a new mom to her daughter. Visit her website www.PTSDwhoMe.com

Chapter 24

In Flows Forgiveness:
How to Melt a Frozen Heart

Kim Harmon

ho is that woman?" I asked as I looked in the mirror. I was forty-two years old and the CEO of a successful healthcare company, but all I could see was a battered child trapped in the body of a grown woman. I was crazed and anxious, running on a gerbil wheel of responsibilities and continuing the cycle of abuse in my life by driving myself mercilessly. The awards, credentials, and high public profile I had achieved were all nothing next to the pain I was trying to hide.

As a child, I had hidden in closets, starting when I was four. It was the only way to avoid the drunken beatings my stepfather gave my mother. I knew if I hid long enough he would forget about me. The family rule was "What happens in the house stays in the house," so I never thought of reaching out for help. I pretended everything was fine, and on the outside I looked happy. Only I knew I felt stone-cold inside. *A layer of ice started to form around my heart.*

As a teenager I was a popular honor roll student at a private Catholic school. But I hated leaving the safety of St. Mary's at the end of each day. At night fear engulfed me—for the lives of my mother, my sister, and me. My stepfather was in and out of jail for years, and my Sunday afternoons were spent visiting him or doing homework in the bars where my mother worked. Everyone adored my mother, Sandra Mae. She was a tall, attractive blonde, who never minded the smokiness and the bloody bar fights the way my younger sister and I did. *The ice around my heart was getting thicker.*

My mom passed away the summer after my freshman year from an infection she got from sharing needles. In her struggle with her own feelings of unworthiness, she had found comfort in heroin. She was only thirty-four. I was devastated. At Mom's funeral, my biological father showed up out of nowhere and invited my sister and me to come live with his new family. He had left us when I was two, so imagine how excited I was at fourteen to finally get the Christmas gift I had dreamed of my whole childhood: I was going to be Daddy's little girl! But no. He had other intentions and they were not pure. Within three months of our move to his house, the emotional and sexual abuse began. *My heart froze solid.*

I was filled with shame and anger, and I hated my mother for choosing her addiction over me almost as much as I hated my father for committing what I felt was the most unspeakable act. But life went on, and, two children and a broken marriage later, I was still frozen inside. I had married for security—I knew it the night before my wedding, but I didn't listen to the inner voice telling me to call it off. And the end of a bad marriage wasn't the end of my woes. The successful business I had built suddenly came to a halt. I found myself closing its doors and going through four years of shareholder litigation and bankruptcy filings, all because I had chosen the wrong partner in business, as well.

I was angry at myself for making bad decisions and not listening to my inner voice. I had lost everything: my marriage, my business, and, in the effort to save my company, even my savings for my children's college educations. I had hit rock bottom and was deeply humiliated. I lived alone, and in my mind's eye, I was curled up like a fetus at the bottom of a rocky mountain. All I could manage to do was start praying. And praying. Every day I spent time praying and meditating and asking God what I was supposed to do.

Time passed, and I began to get the idea that I was being called to write a book, but I didn't even know what it was about. The idea persisted, so I decided to take a workshop that would help me get clearer on my vision. I scraped together the money to fly out to the West Coast for the Enlightened Bestseller Mastermind Experience, a workshop created for just this purpose. At the end of the first day there I wrote out two questions, each on its own index card. On one I wrote: *What is the book about?* On the other: *Who am I writing it for?* I held the cards and said a prayer, then gently placed them under my pillow and went to sleep.

At four a.m. I suddenly woke up. I knew the book was about forgiveness! I sat up in bed, turned on the light, and reached for my notebook and pen. I knew that forgiveness was my way out of the darkness I had been in for so long. And if I could find my way through it and write about it, maybe I could help many others who needed to find forgiveness too.

At last, I had my answers! For the first time in my life, I had a glimmer of understanding of where I had come from and where I was going. I saw that my suffering wasn't wasted, and that I could take my experience and share it with others for their healing.

I started writing about forgiveness, and as I did, I began to sense the higher power that was taking control of my life—or had always been in control of my life! I completely surrendered to it. I said to God, "I want what You want. My will is Your will, and I will do what You want me to do. Just, please, show me the way."

I knew I was at the very bottom and there was only one way to go: *up!* I begged God to take away anyone in my life who was not helping me stay on my path and bring me those who would. I made a promise to God and to myself that if I was shown the way, I would follow it. I trusted I would be led…but I had no idea how fast it all would all happen! *Something was shifting deep inside me. My heart was getting warmer.*

The course ended and I flew back to New York. At the airport, the man I was in a relationship with was irritated that my flight had been delayed. I, in turn, was feeling anything but love. During the ride to his house where I had been visiting, the little voice inside me was saying it was time to say good-bye. Suddenly, right then and there in the car, I told him I was leaving. Back at his place, now full of strength, I put my bags in my little Subaru and made the five-hour drive to my home in Massachusetts. It was scary to be on my own again, but deep down I was glad. *This time I listened to that voice.*

Things started happening so fast I could hardly catch my breath at times. Before the trip I had been looking for a new position and fighting for a settlement with my previous employer. Within three days of returning home I received a great offer to teach nursing part-time at a local university. Wow, I hadn't even sent them my resume! They had found me! I love teaching, and this income would pay the bills while I wrote the book.

By this time I was diligently praying and meditating for a minimum of an hour and a half every morning, often waking at four a.m. to start. The book was coming together as I was gaining an understanding of the importance of forgiveness. And the pieces of the puzzle of my life—my relationships with my father, my mother, my ex-husband, my ex–business partner, and myself—were coming together, too. I started taking each relationship, one at a time, and working on the task of forgiving the person—just within my own heart, not needing to reach out to them.

Then the miracles came: I was smiling. Yes, me…smiling! I was feeling happy! What on earth was going on? My heart was warm, and the gifts it held were coming through. *I was thawing out.*

The changes started coming, little by little. Some people left my life, while others showed up. Before long, I was surrounded with caring individuals, full of kindness and generosity, who were keeping me on my path. I found myself leaning on them because this new feeling of letting go was very scary. I felt I was in the midst of a physical transformation as well as a spiritual one. I felt like a butterfly breaking out of a chrysalis and realized that I was making the transformation from a physical healer to a spiritual healer. *My heart was flowing in love.*

When I finally emerged, I knew I had knowledge that could change people's lives. So, let me share with you what I've learned so far about forgiveness.

The Four Steps to Start the Flow of Forgiveness

Here are four simple steps that have made a huge difference in my life. My hope is that they will transform your life as beautifully as they have transformed mine.

1. Downsize your ego by letting go of your fear

The number-one reason people choose not to forgive is because they're afraid of humiliation. This fear feeds the ego with thoughts like, *I'll look like a fool if I say I'm sorry,* or *Why should I say I'm sorry? I was right and they were wrong!* By consciously rejecting such thoughts, you can minimize your ego and shift from fear to a heart-centered place of love. You can also release any attachment you have to potential outcomes, let go of what other people think you should do or say, and give up your belief that you are in control of the outcome.

"How do I do these difficult things?" you ask? There is only one way: You must call on your divine source for help and allow divine love to flow through your heart, as you set your intention to do them. Realize that it's by *letting go* of your fears that you gain freedom. *Surrender* those fears—lay them down and walk away from them—and trust that you will be stronger without them. This is something you'll do many, many times, not just once. But it's a practice that will make you stronger and freer every time you do it. Be prepared to be surprised at how your life begins to open up as you release the bonds that have constricted it until now.

2. Pay attention to the pain of nonforgiveness

Take care to notice all the signs of your lack of forgiveness of others that are around you and within you. Make note of the times during your day when you are triggered by something to feel hurt, angry, or sad. It could be an interaction with someone, a song on the radio, a smell, a memory. How does it make your body feel? Tense, stressed, nauseous? Recognize that the pain you feel—and may have been feeling for a long time—is due to unresolved issues, which often require forgiveness to heal.

That pain will eventually lead you to a place where you want to forgive, or perhaps ask for forgiveness. And sometimes it leads you to forgive yourself. As you do, you'll see the pain retreat and what's left is the joy that is your natural state.

3. Be still and listen

Listen for the truth within you—and listen carefully. Create time in your daily schedule to be silent because in silence you can hear the wisdom you already have within you. It's only when you quiet your mind and put your ego down for a nap that you can hear the voice of your inner, wiser self. This is the place where you are connected to your conscience and to deeper, more powerful levels of consciousness.

It can be for as little as ten minutes a day, but the trick is in committing to do it every day. In this ten minutes, pick one relationship that you want to restore, one person you are struggling to forgive. Tune in to the stillness within you—the deep reservoir of your awareness—and from this quiet, open space, send this person love, from your heart to theirs. They will feel it without knowing what it is, and doing this will prepare you for the final step.

4. Practice forgiveness

Follow the signs you noticed in step 2, and choose one of the people you identified in step 3. Then take these action steps:

a. Call on your divine source to help your heart soften and flow in love as you visualize the person.

b. Say these words, internally or out loud: "I bless you, I forgive you, and I release you."

c. Picture your heart opening and flowing in love, and then send that love to the person you are forgiving.

d. Repeat as needed, over time, until you know in your heart you have forgiven the person. Each time you do this you will feel lighter, and your relief will grow.

This process is simple but it isn't easy. You have to have the support of your divine source at each step to give you the strength to release your grip on the feelings you've been carrying. No doubt you have many good reasons to have those feelings! Nonetheless, they're only hurting you. And they're probably hurting everyone around you, too. They're walls around your heart, blocking your light from shining out.

So, be not afraid! Be glad every time you can humbly say, to yourself or others, silently or out loud, "I forgive you." The act of forgiving is your gift to yourself, as well as the other person. It frees you from pain every single time you do it.

• • •

You can transform yourself and everyone around you, little by little, by using these four steps. And as you continue to integrate them into your life, you'll see changes everywhere. After a while, you may not even recognize your life and your relationships, they look so different. But I can guarantee that you'll love what you see!

Forgiveness is the path to living in love and freedom. Whatever traumas you may have endured, and however icy you fear your heart may have become, through forgiveness that ice will melt, and you will become the loving and happy person you were meant to be. Through forgiveness, you'll soon be flowing with the divine current in the beautiful river of life.

Kimberly Marie Harmon, RN is a nursing professor, entrepreneur, and CEO of Life Enterprises, as well as a keynote speaker on the topic of forgiveness for religious organizations, women's groups, and prisons. Drawing on her experience as a successful CEO in the healthcare field, she provides consulting to top healthcare executives to help them lead from the place of their Original Heart®.

Kim is the founder of Project ForGIFT®, a not-for-profit division of her ministry, which is committed to sharing the ForGIFT Pathway of Forgiveness and the message of divine mercy. She has two children and lives in New England. To contact Kim for US and international speaking, workshops, or consulting services, visit her at www.KimberlyMarieHarmon.com.

Chapter 25

In the Presence of Ducks:
How Agreements Shape Our Lives

Candace Pedicord

"Mom, are you crying?"

My eyes were filled with tears. "The duck…," I said, pointing. My daughter and I were in a small café, fresh coffee steaming in front of us. A father and two small girls were putting on their coats behind us. I shared what I'd just seen.

The father announced to his two young daughters, maybe two and a half and four years old, that it was time to leave. He held out a coat. The younger one hesitated, confused. She held a small, yellow duck in her tiny hand. In order to put on the coat, she needed to put down the duck. She looked at the duck, then at her father. She put the duck on the floor, picked it up, put it back down, picked it up. Her wide eyes never left it. Her father continued to hold out the coat. Finally, she put down the duck and turned away, for an instant.

Her sister took the duck.

And I burst into tears.

In that moment, all of *my* "duck moments" surfaced, times when I made a decision to trust and then had to let go of my ideas of what was right or fair. I felt the injustice of life.

Who I am in the presence of ducks matters. Life is not *designed* to be fair. It is designed to give me ducks. It is designed to challenge me into finding my potential. I was grateful to feel the raw pain of that moment. It was temporary and enlightening. It reminded me that my stories have the capacity to trap me or free me. In truth, I am being guided, at all times, by something greater than my stories. Life happens *for* me, not *to* me.

The following stories approach living from three different perspectives with one thing in common: Each is an example of how to create an agreement with yourself or God about how to live your life. Sure, there are ducks. But let them fly into your foundation of personal responsibility and trust in something greater than your expectations. Then, they are just ducks. And you find out who *you* are.

Enjoy!

The Hole (Whole) Story

> *The power behind taking responsibility for your actions lies in putting an end to negative thought patterns. You no longer dwell on what went wrong or focus on whom you are going to blame. You don't waste time building roadblocks to your success. Instead, you are set free and can now focus on succeeding.*
>
> —**Lorii Myers**, author and entrepreneur

It is amazing how quickly my thoughts can imprison me. A recent breakup opened the ground underneath my feet and swallowed me whole. Easy thoughts of comfort and companionship were replaced by entire treatises of "this can't be happening" and "why now" and "if only" and "I can't do this" and "I don't want this" and "I don't know what to do." The good times became even more beautiful now that they were gone.

I felt as if I'd fallen into a hole.

I watched my self-talk increase. "I thought everything was fine." "I don't want to be alone." "This shouldn't have happened." And then the final blow, "And yet, here I am. *Again.*"

I think I am busy figuring things out, but I'm not. I'm just wandering around bumping up against a limited set of thoughts that will do nothing to help me. I know better, but I do it anyway.

The help I actually need is found in these three steps:

1. Acknowledge I am in a hole. I am *in a hole.*
2. Decide to get out.
3. Get out.

All three are essential.

1. The hole has nothing to do with the breakup. The hole is about my focus on what *isn't* working instead of what *could be* working. Furthermore, it is my *agreement* to be in the hole that is the real problem. My acceptance of the *hole* reality makes it my *whole* reality. Is this truly where I want to be? And for how long?
2. As I fully comprehend that I am going nowhere and that the days outside my hole will come and go as I watch helplessly from this sorry perspective, something kicks in. I feel a level of commitment deep in my soul, in alignment with the universal principle of *move*. I decide to *get out*. Seamlessly, all the resources of the Universe begin to guide me. A random phone call from an old friend. A movie about starting over. A client who is going through a breakup and needs clarity. An invitation to join a new

yoga studio. *My clarity around* deciding *to get out miraculously creates options.*

3. I have the awareness; I have the clarity. I even have options. And yet, there is something familiar and even comfortable about being stuck. I hesitate. But my soul, my future, the potential of what is waiting for me beckons … and I courageously make a choice. My freedom trumps my suffering. I climb out, one action at a time.

We all fall in holes. We all have fears and limiting beliefs. We have gone through the day with bad hair or a rip in our pants. There are bad photos of all of us. We have said stupid things and hurt those we love. The whole reality is that holes teach us to climb out of our thoughts and into our souls. There is no place I'd rather be.

The Clementine Principle:
Create Agreements instead of Expectations

My core belief is that if you're complaining about something for more than three minutes, two minutes ago you should have done something about it.
  —**Caitlin Moran**, author and English broadcaster

One of my most cherished companions is a young bamboo given to me four years ago. It sits in my office, a silent and beautiful expression of love. It grows in the presence of the work I do, with the sunlight streaming in and resting in the water I bring to it. Unlike the wild bamboo that can stealthily take over a backyard, it emerges in a way that gives me time to enlarge its container gradually, four pots over four years. Our relationship is based in love and grounded in what is present. It asks me to pay attention. I am able to do that. Bamboos just grow. We live in harmony and peace, giving what we are able to give of ourselves without expectation of anything in return.

I will not betray this agreement I have made with my companion.

And, as much as I love it, it is not an orange tree.

Occasionally, I will point that out to a client. As much as he might want oranges, in this moment, no amount of wishing and cajoling and blaming and disappointment will make the bamboo produce a fruit. He can stare at it, glare at it, roll his eyes, and turn his back. He can become depressed and sullen, make sarcastic remarks and withdraw his attention. He can eventually give up on it and resign himself to a life without oranges. He can hold on to his resentment and feel his energy deflate and become agitated whenever he "has" to water it, even though it refuses to give him the thing he wants most.

What is the difference between asking the bamboo to give me oranges and asking another human being to do or be what I need? Who am I to think that another should be different so I am more comfortable?

One dear client brought that message to heart and now carries what she calls the Clementine Stone, a small orange stone that reminds her of clementine oranges and helps her to remember that she creates the agitation she feels when others do not live up to her expectations.

The Clementine Principle holds this foundational truth: No one and no thing is responsible for your emotional or spiritual well-being. A Clementine Moment is each moment you are aware of needing someone else or something else to behave differently so you are more comfortable. Just because you *want* someone to love you or hear you or be generous with you does not mean that he or she is supposed to do it. There is no agreement; there is only your unrealistic expectation.

If you want something, make an agreement with yourself. Agree to *create* it instead of trying to *get* it. That includes love, wealth, health, opportunity, clients, friendships, intimacy, freedom, adventure, and peace. The love and appreciation you generate will create more love and appreciation from everyone around you. The tithing and generosity you offer the world will come back to you tenfold. The energy of service you put out into the world will fill your heart and satisfy the deepest longing you have for making a difference.

And, if you want orange juice, grow an orange tree, preferably where the backyard bamboo will not take it over. A bamboo is, after all, a bamboo.

He's Yours: Choosing Love instead of Worry

You can only have one first-born child. You may love all your children deeply and with passion, but there is something unique about the first-born.
—**Raymond E. Feist**, author of fantasy fiction

Amen.

Soon after my son's second birthday, my agreement regarding motherhood shifted dramatically.

My precious little boy did not seem to understand the limitations of his perfect little body. His deeply loving nature was also fully willful and stubborn, and I found myself following him rather than guiding him. For all of his tenderness and wanting to be close, his nature was to run and charge and slip and fall. He depended on me to keep him safe, and yet I already had thirteen of his stitches tucked away in an envelope.

I had to renegotiate my relationship with him before he got much bigger. At least at two, I could still pluck him off the dog and deposit him in a high chair.

I was learning that mother love is not enough when a soul wants to explore everything.

I grew up learning that "mother" and "worry" were inextricably linked. After all, my mother had modeled the "right" way to do things.

You instill enough fear in your young, so they will avoid dangerous things like skydiving and anger, and then find a way to enjoy life from the sidelines.

For some reason, I bought into this strategy, but it clearly was not going to work with this beautiful boy. I was on a crash course, literally, of learning how to let go.

So, one summer morning in a moment of absolute clarity, watching him run and fall and run and trip, I turned him over to God.

"God," I said, "he's yours. I'll clothe him and feed him and love him and guide him and get him to school and take him to parks. I'll make sure he knows who You are, and I'll teach him manners and courtesy and honesty and the value of working hard. He'll have consequences and opportunities and hugs and kisses, and I'll share as much of what I know and value as I can with him. But, in the end and starting now, he's yours. I can't keep him safe. I can't keep him out of the emergency room. I can't limit him and deny him the chance to explore this beautiful world you've created for him. He's on his own path. Help guide me in raising him, and I'll do everything I can. But, he's your son. Thank you."

I do not know where that moment came from or how it settled into my body like a blanket over a sleeping baby. I just knew, clearly and fully, a sense of peace.

Clarity will do that. Intention. Commitment. Reality. Surrender.

Amazingly, although I had no knowledge of this at the time, the Bible expressly states, "Every firstborn boy is to be set apart as holy to the Lord." God was all in even before I asked.

Here is the important thing about my agreement with God. I did not ask God to keep him safe. In fact, I did not ask God to do much. I simply said what *I* was willing to do and then added, "He's yours." God is *always* all in, just waiting for me to be clear.

You are not meant to worry your way through life. My decision to turn him over was my simple acknowledgement that he was already in a relationship with this magnificent Universe, and I was deliberately and lovingly stepping out of the way. I found I had a choice about how to live my life and how to let him live his.

I was in awe, really, when I was given, in that moment, a different way to be. Honestly, it didn't even seem like my idea. It felt like a decision that was downloaded into my heart and voice, and I just let it flow. In a single, life-changing moment, I chose love instead of worry. Since then, I have been the voice of reason but not the voice of fear.

Skip ahead to June, 2004. Fourteen thousand feet. A bright, sunny afternoon. I am crouched in the back of a small Cessna, unable to hear anything but the roar of the wind through the open door. I grin at my now eighteen-year-old son kneeling a few feet from me. He looks concerned and points to a strap at my shoulder. "You're not fastened in!" he shouts, and then he's gone, dropped through the door into the endlessly blue sky.

We are celebrating his birthday and my new life as a single mom by skydiving. We've chosen the tandem route, falling at 120 miles per hour attached to an instructor. Except I'm not completely attached to mine. Thank you, Mike. How beautifully our roles have shifted. My instructor fastens us properly, I take a deep breath, and we, too, tumble out into the void.

I'm sorry, Mom, but it was amazing. And I'm still alive. I'm *more* alive. And I got to experience life *with* my son.

Fast forward again to my twenty-six-year-old as he sits in the back of my car holding his breath. "What are you doing?" I ask, peering at him in the rearview mirror. "Training," he explained. "Sometimes, when you surf, the waves pin you down against the bottom, and you may not be able to get to the surface for a few minutes." He grinned.

I sigh, smile, and shake my head, remembering my original agreement to turn him over. "He's yours," I say softly, again, and continue to peek back at him, grateful that he is doing his best to stay safe in his world, as I am in mine.

Live, love, play. Stay out of holes and jump out of airplanes. Make agreements with God, your choices, and your actions. You are loved and guided and held accountable by the most beautiful love there is. Enjoy!

Candace Pedicord, MS, coaches from the heart. She is an energy healer, intuitive, and interfaith minister. She is direct and loving and challenges her clients to move beyond familiar beliefs and patterns. "Life happens for you, not to you" provides the framework for deep personal inquiry and focused action. She is dedicated to the alignment of spiritual and human effort through her trademarked SpiritYOUality process and coaching. "Your highest calling is to serve and your greatest challenge is to embrace your fears. If you are willing to do both, let's talk. Your transformation lives in dedicated, consistent and courageous action." For a deep and powerful conversation, connect with Candace at spiritedlifecoaching.com.

Chapter 26

Your Sacred Purpose: Put Your Personal Power and Passion to Work Now!

Raven Sinclaire

To be human is to become visible while carrying what is hidden as a gift to others.

—David White

W ho's there?" I whispered in the darkness. My heart was racing. Shivering in the pink flannel nightgown my aunt had sent me for my eighth birthday, I stood frozen on the attic stairs, halfway between the ordinary and the unknown, and waited for an answer. The soft voice spoke again: "You are able to walk into the darkness. You can change the dark to light and carry it back to them. That is what you do. That is who you are."

"Who's there?" was a question I was used to asking. The answers came in various ways. Sometimes a voice, sometimes a thought, sometimes a strong pull that would take me to a place where there was more information, like in a scavenger hunt. My mother, struggling with her own denial, would tell me the voices I heard were my angels talking.

My earliest memory of spirit communication took place when I was two years old. My mother remembered it too and often told the story over the years. She was in the grocery store when an elderly man approached her and asked if she was Mrs. Seright and I was her daughter. She said yes, and he told her that I called him on the phone every day. He said that I only talked for a couple of minutes and would start by telling him that my mother was out watering the flowers. My mother was horrified. She apologized to the man and said she would make sure I didn't do it again.

"Oh, no!" he said, realizing his mistake. "Please don't make her stop! My wife died a year ago and she's the only person who calls."

I still remember my toddler-self pushing the chair over to the wall-mounted phone and talking quietly so no one would hear. Sometimes my mother would catch me and think I was only pretending, so I would hang up. Now she was mystified. How in the world could a two-year-old dial the same number every day?

What Mom didn't know was that it was the man's dead wife who told me the number to dial, and she also gave me messages for him, secrets that only the two of them shared. That's why it was so important to the man that I continue to call. I was keeping his wife alive for him in the only way he had.

The burden of this gift was apparent at an early age, but the value of it—and the reward—became clear only much later in life.

It didn't occur to me for many years that these out-of-the-ordinary experiences could ever morph into my livelihood. When adults asked what I wanted to be when I grew up, I would never have thought to say, "I want to talk to people's angels and spirit guides to help them live their highest and best life." Thank goodness! I probably would have been hospitalized!

But as a result, as I grew into adulthood, I struggled with finding my perfect vocation. No career was a fit, and the way the spirit world so often bled into my physical world sometimes made me think there had been a slip-up at my birth, and somehow I had come in unfinished. I would often ponder the question of my life's purpose, while responding to whispers from the spirit realm with "Be quiet and let me think!" I felt a need for nourishment deep in my soul, and an even greater need to *give* nourishment and be of service to others.

Does my story ring any bells for you? Have you been ignoring some persistent clues as to what you should *really* be doing with your life? Does the voice in your head ever nag at you with suggestions that you brush aside as impractical or ridiculous? And meanwhile, do you languish in work you find unsatisfying?

It wasn't until years later that, as a single parent trying to bring in an extra paycheck, I began to consider the idea of making money from these lifelong gifts. I was working as the communications director for a small company in 2007 when I saw an ad for an unusual job: a "ghost tour guide." I called them and found it was for a popular walking tour through historic downtown Asheville. Soon I was leading these tours and beginning the nightly walk with the disclosure, "Actually, folks, I do see ghosts—and talk to ghosts. It's an ability I've had my entire life."

People's eyes get really big when you say that. But the great thing was…they loved it! In this context the confession was entertaining and just edgy enough to be a thrill. And for me, this job was an awakening to a new world. For the first time in my life, I was not only coming clean with my ability, I was actually promoting my own little superpower. I didn't have a perplexing secret to hide; I had a fun and useful gift to share and enjoy! This small step began to change my life.

I wonder…might you have a gift that you've been overlooking? Do you brush aside a talent as not special or useful or serious enough to be worth mentioning? Is it something you've even been embarrassed by? Can you imagine looking at it in another way?

Word got out about my abilities, and calls began coming in. Most people asked me to come to their haunted businesses or homes to see what was going on. In the beginning I turned them down because I already had my hands full, working two jobs and raising children. Then one day, a woman I'll call Diane said, "I'll pay you anything you want. I don't want to leave my home and I'm desperate for some relief." My head started spinning. *Whoa, I can charge for this?* I seriously hadn't thought of that as a possibility. This was just a knack I was born with. I hadn't gone to school for it or taken any workshops to develop it. It just seemed too easy to be worth being compensated for.

But I did take Diane up on her offer, and I charged her a fee that made it worth my time, though just barely. When I visited her home the next day, three different spirits confronted me. They told me their full names and a few other details, but one thing was odd: None of them had ever lived in this house. It was clear that they were more attached to Diane than the house. I did a clearing and the activity subsided.

Diane was very grateful—but there was more. Months later, she contacted me and told me she had become lost in a daydream while driving and had ended up stopping at an old cemetery that she had never known existed. Feeling as if someone were leading her, she walked through the cemetery and found herself stopping at two gravestones. To her amazement, they were inscribed with two of the names I had given her months before! Her research into them eventually revealed the third name as well, and more research revealed that that person was, in fact, connected to her lineage.

Even more thrilling was that the work that Diane did to uncover these people's stories facilitated a deep healing for her and broke her old patterns of addiction and disease. Through later sessions we had, she was able to identify the tug of her ancestors from as far back as early childhood when they would come to her in dreams. She was very grateful to be able to finally begin to understand and deal with these underlying issues in her life.

More work came to me, and at the same time, one of my longtime passions, women's empowerment, was also brought into the picture. A mentor miraculously showed up and began apprenticing me to facilitate women's circles that involved deep inner work to remove barriers to wholeness and often help the women uncover…you guessed it…their life purpose. My passion for helping women found the perfect expression through the facilitation of women's circles, and my now treasured little superpower of spirit communication greatly enhances my work.

For years I was pursuing various careers from the outside in, rather than from the inside out. I looked out into the world and didn't see a need for my gifts, so I made do with something else. But when I finally listened to the inner call of those gifts and created a career from the inside out, my life's work began to fall into place. When I merged my passion (empowering women) with my inner power (spirit communication), I began to fulfill one of my purposes (women's circles and workshops).

Eventually, I also offered shamanic sessions with clients, serving as an intermediary between spirit and matter to help them live their highest and best life. It's not surprising that many of the men and women I work with in shamanic sessions are looking for their place in the world, whether they are twenty-two or sixty-two. I have clients who went to school to be architects, accountants, or teachers and they've had long careers, sometimes fulfilling, sometimes not. Now their spirits are calling for them to create from the inside out, allowing their spirit to inform their work, rather than letting the world define their purpose for them. When we start to give reverence to our inner superpowers and pursue our passions, doors begin to open and answers begin to flow.

Getting in touch with your soul's purpose begins with simple steps. I recommend starting with a few journaling exercises, given below.

Imagine the Life You Were Meant to Live

Did you once dream of a life different from the one you're living now? What was it like? What did you picture yourself doing? What do you picture yourself doing now, if you could do anything you wanted? Take a few minutes to settle down and allow thoughts and emotions to flow, and then write about these questions and about the life you feel you were truly meant to live.

Uncover Your Innate Wisdom or Superpower

Dr. Christiane Northrup says that little girls feel their life's calling at the age of eleven, and I'm sure it's similar for boys. Take a trip through the pages of your memories back to your childhood, and write down the memories that come, without overthinking or analyzing. Just let them flow. Pay special attention to the aspects of yourself that others complimented or sought out. These may be your neglected superpowers. Also write about the secret desires you never shared. We often protect our greatest dreams and our most powerful gifts from ridicule by keeping them hidden.

Start to Sing Your Soul's Unique Song

Jot down your interests and passions. This is different from your innate powers. Make a list of those too. Your passions create the paths on which your powers will travel. In my case, one of my passions is women's empowerment, and my power is a connection to spirit, or other dimensions. Another of my passions is writing, which also draws on that power to share knowledge of other dimensions. Your interests and passions are your guide to how to use your power in the world for your own growth and that of others. Look at your two lists and write about ways you could use your powers to fulfill your passions.

Magic Happens When You Begin Your Sacred Work

Based on what you discovered in these three exercises, write about what you would like your life to look like:

- How would you feel?
- What kinds of activities would make up your day?
- Where would you live?

Below this, list your passions on one side and your powers on the other, and begin to be open to the magic of the universe to find a way to merge the two into your sacred work. You may already see a road map to marry your passion and power, or you may receive clues over the next weeks or months. Know that the timing is not always as we hope but always perfect.

• • •

It's my wish that everyone can make a good living doing the work they feel called to do. For that to happen, you have to (1) put the right value on your services and (2) use good business sense in developing your business. I've already mentioned my struggle with the first point, and I know I'm not alone. But this is crazy! When you merge your passion and power into purpose, the result is a transformational offering that has great value. When someone needs surgery, they don't look for the cheapest doctor out there or the one who's running a special. Their well-being is way more important than that. The same thing goes with goods and services that will transform lives. Value your calling, and others will as well.

As for the second point, it doesn't tarnish your spiritual gifts in any way to use good marketing skills to build a viable business for yourself. Here are my top suggestions:

1. It's always important in any kind of creative or spiritual work to gather with others and form alliances. I began offering shamanic sessions to friends and also to others who had contacts or associations I didn't have. Word spreads quickly this way, and referrals are your greatest resource.
2. Build an email list by offering a free newsletter, article reprint, recording, or interview online.
3. Schedule free local talks and come prepared to gather email addresses and promote services or products that you offer for a fee.
4. Remember always to be authentic and work from your heart, even when dealing with business matters.

I often remember the words I heard when I was caught in between worlds on the stairs, and these days they finally ring true: "You are able to walk into the darkness (see what is hidden). You can change the dark to light and carry it back to them (bring the vision to those who can't see it). That is what you do. That is who you are."

When your sacred purpose begins to emerge, you'll realize that it was there all along, waiting patiently for you to dare to imagine you could live an abundant and valued life, following your passion and putting your unique power to work in the world. This is your gift to the world, and the support that flows to you from giving it is your birthright. Believe that you can spend every day living your passions

Printed in the USA
CPSIA information can be
at www.ICGtesting.com
JSHW021500220424
61660JS00006B/34

well-being is way more important than that. The same thing goes with goods and services that will transform lives. Value your calling, and others will as well.

As for the second point, it doesn't tarnish your spiritual gifts in any way to use good marketing skills to build a viable business for yourself. Here are my top suggestions:

1. It's always important in any kind of creative or spiritual work to gather with others and form alliances. I began offering shamanic sessions to friends and also to others who had contacts or associations I didn't have. Word spreads quickly this way, and referrals are your greatest resource.

2. Build an email list by offering a free newsletter, article reprint, recording, or interview online.

3. Schedule free local talks and come prepared to gather email addresses and promote services or products that you offer for a fee.

4. Remember always to be authentic and work from your heart, even when dealing with business matters.

I often remember the words I heard when I was caught in between worlds on the stairs, and these days they finally ring true: "You are able to walk into the darkness (see what is hidden). You can change the dark to light and carry it back to them (bring the vision to those who can't see it). That is what you do. That is who you are."

When your sacred purpose begins to emerge, you'll realize that it was there all along, waiting patiently for you to dare to imagine you could live an abundant and valued life, following your passion and putting your unique power to work in the world. This is your gift to the world, and the support that flows to you from giving it is your birthright. Believe that you can spend every day living your passions and giving your gift to the world! It's what you're here to do.

Raven Sinclaire is a speaker, shamanic counselor, and author whose passion is helping others tap into their own spiritual guidance to heal and transform. She is a facilitator of the Shamanic Priestess Path™ and Magdalene Mysteries™ and creator of the Living Intuitively Now™ training course.

Raven teaches the power of utilizing intuition to women's groups and corporate audiences and is the author of Pamper Your Way to Prosperity: From Barely Surviving to Happy and Thriving. *Raven also leads sacred tours to Scotland, Ireland, and France. She is the mother of three grown children and lives in Asheville, North Carolina. Visit www.ravensinclaire.com.*

Enlightened Bestseller
Mastermind Experience

Are you currently writing a transformational book or planning to in the near future? Or have you already self-published a self-help book and sales havev not met your expectations? Imagine what a difference it could make if you received guidance from a team who have collectively produced eight *New York Times* bestsellers and sold over fifteen million books.

This could be the opportunity you've been waiting for! We are in the process of handpicking a select group of authors to work intimately with to create their bestselling books and online platforms.

In fact, we've personally mentored all of the contributing authors in this book. And we're proud to say that all of them have published, or will soon publish, a self-help book. Our protégés have also relied on our guidance to build their speaking businesses as well as create products and programs based on their book's message so they can reach even more people.

If you have a transformational message to share with the world and could benefit from expert guidance on writing, publishing, and promoting your book as well as building your platform as an author, we invite you to visit *www.enlightenedbestseller.com* and see if this could be a good fit with your goals and aspirations.

To your bestseller!

—**Janet Bray Attwood, Marci Shimoff,**
Chris Attwood, and Geoff Affleck